What readers are saying about *Never Retire*...

"Everyone over age thirty-five should read this book. *Never Retire* skillfully combines financial planning strategies with a refreshing perspective on preparing to make the most of our retirement years. If you want an exciting, financially independent future, Dan Benson will show you how to turn your dreams into reality."

—DENNIS E. MEANS,
Certified Financial Planner, Financial Services Network

"When Dan Benson speaks, people should listen. Few authors are more insightful than Dan when dealing with practical issues of life. He provides wise counsel."

—JOSH MCDOWELL

"Dan Benson is on to something big here! He has a great philosophy of reinvesting in life rather than retiring. His book has the potential of rallying men and women of experience to great causes, which can change our culture."

—MERRILL OSTER,
Oster Family Limited Partnership

"Proverbs exhorts us to prepare for the future as the ant does. Most of us do so like slugs! Dan Benson sets forth wise and practical principles that, if followed, will assure we are not on the dole or in the doldrums in our sunset years."

—LARRY W. POLAND, PH.D.,
Chairman and CEO, Mastermedia International, Inc.

"*Never Retire* is an inspiration for how your later years can have so much more meaning. Benson gives practical steps to defining and achieving your dreams."

—BRUCE JOHNSON,
NextLevel Leadership

Never grow old. Just grow.
Never retreat. Rejuvenate.
Never give in. Give back.

NEVER RETIRE

How to
Secure Financial Freedom
and
Live Out Your Dreams

DAN BENSON

WORD PUBLISHING
NASHVILLE
A Thomas Nelson Company

Published in association with the literary agency of Alive Communications, Inc., 1465 Kelly Johnson Blvd., Suite 320, Colorado Springs, Colorado, 80920.

Library of Congress Cataloging-in-Publication Data

Benson, Dan
    Never retire / Dan Benson
      p. cm.
    ISBN 0-8499-3772-8
    1. Retirement—United States—Planning. 2. Retirement income—United States—Planning. 3. Finance. Personal. I. Title.
    HQ1063.2.U6B46 1999
    646.7'9—dc21   99-39399
                                                                    CIP

Printed in the United States of America
99 00 01 02 03 04 05 BVG 6 5 4 3 2 1

To Mom and Dad Benson,
who gave me the true wealth of love, nurture,
faith in God, and a good name.
and
To Mom and Dad Means,
who gave me true riches in Kathy,
and who love me as their own.

CONTENTS

PART TWO:
THE SEVEN PILLARS OF FINANCIALLY INDEPENDENT RETIREMENT

PART THREE:
THRIVING IN THE NEW RETIREMENT

ACKNOWLEDGMENTS

M y special thanks to Dennis E. Means, CFP (certified financial planner), who reviewed the manuscript, checked my numbers, and provided constructive feedback. Since 1979, Dennis has been helping people with personal retirement planning, tax planning, estate planning, and investment portfolio design. He is part owner of Financial Services Network, Inc., a Registered Investment Advisory firm in Denver, Colorado. To talk with him about personal financial planning assistance, contact Dennis E. Means, CFP, 3801 East Florida Avenue, Suite 610, Denver, CO 80210. Phone: (303) 300-0206. Fax: (303) 300-0160.

Thanks also to Greg Johnson of Alive Communications and Mark Sweeney of Word Publishing for sharing my excitement for this project and steering it toward reality. To Ami McConnell, senior editor, for her expertise, patience, and caring spirit as she guided the manuscript to press. To Randy Kady of ProGrafix for his computer graphic skills on the "Seven Pillars" illustration and on several charts and graphs. To Candace McMahan for her keen editorial eye. And to Word's entire staff for helping spread the word that our someday "retirement" should not be a time of resignation, but of rejuvenation.

Most of all, my love and appreciation to my sweet wife of twenty-five years, who guarded my writing time and provided encouragement, nourishment, and a gentle prod toward the computer when I preferred to go out and play. I still cannot comprehend why God thinks I deserve such a blessing as Kathy, but I'm sure not going to argue with him.

—Dan Benson

ONE

NEVER RETIRE?

Make the most of the rest of your life.

If you scan magazine headlines or watch TV news shows, you can't miss the drumbeat. It once was soft, distant. But it drums louder each day, and closer.

The drumbeat is retirement. *Your* retirement.

Someday, like it or not, either your company or your inner clock will tell you it's time to close the shutters on the work you've pursued all your adult life. Suddenly, you will be *on your own* for the next twenty to thirty years. And twenty to thirty years is a long time.

What will you do with your days?

How will you support yourself when the paychecks suddenly stop?

How will you stay young at heart, strong of body, keen of mind?

How will you make the most of the rest of your life?

Indeed, it's hard to miss the publicity—or escape the pressure. Especially the financial pressure. Men and women born early in the pre–baby boom decade (1936 to 1945) are just a few years away from traditional retirement age. Following closely is the baby boom generation, our nation's 76 million men and women born between 1946 and 1964. Those born in the early 1950s are within fifteen to twenty years of this major life-change. Those born near the start of the boom are only a decade or so from retirement.

Whatever our time frame, we midlifers are thinking more and more about our age . . . and the future.

At some point we realized that we had already lived one-half of our lives. Sobering. Where did the time go?

We used to think we'd live forever. It's still strange to think about growing old. But it's not as strange now as it was twenty years ago.

It used to be that our bosses, and many of our colleagues, were older than we were. Now more and more of them weren't yet born when JFK was shot. Fewer and fewer of our coworkers saw the first moon landing or know who the Beatles were.

With each passing week we find more gray in our hair, less hair in our hairlines. When we were young, we couldn't wait to be older. Now that we're older, we long to be young.

We vowed as teenagers never to say, "When I was your age . . ." But now we catch ourselves saying just that. We're now the age our parents once were.

My, it all passes so quickly. The Psalmist must have felt the same way when he wrote, "We glide along the tides of time as swiftly as a racing river, and vanish as quickly as a dream" (Psalm 90:5–6, TLB).

We thought we had forever to think about getting old. Now it's just a decade or two away.

The older we get, the faster life goes.

And someday we'll be our parents' age again.

WILL THE MONEY BE THERE
WHEN YOU NEED IT?

We midlifers have also observed our elders—the retired generations—and weighed their retirement realities against our own retirement dreams. Some of our elders thrive; others seem to barely subsist. When our time comes, we'd prefer to thrive. With modern health advances and increased life spans, we may spend as much as *one-third of our lives* in retirement. We realize that, while money is not a be-all and end-all, our laterlife options could be severely limited if we do not build sufficient financial reserves for those twenty to thirty years.

Will we be ready when the steady paycheck is replaced by a gold watch? It's a question more and more of us are asking, and not without good reason. Consider these findings from recent studies:

√ Two-thirds of baby boomers say they often think about their retirement and the money they'll need.

√ Most baby boomers have saved less than $3,000 for retirement.

√ Nearly 60 percent of baby boomers in their forties think they could personally face a retirement-savings crisis.

√ Eighty-two percent of Americans believe that, should baby boomers fail to save adequately, they will need to live with their adult children when they retire.

√ In recent years, only 2 percent of retiring Americans have been able to self-finance this major life-change. Twenty-three percent have continued to work, whether they wanted to or not, to meet basic living expenses. A massive 75 percent could not make ends meet without Social Security or help from their adult children or charitable organizations.

√ Despite assurances from politicians, midlife adults are skeptical that Social Security will be a viable source of support in their senior years, if it's available at all.

√ One-quarter of adults between the ages of thirty-five and sixty-four have not even *begun* to save for their retirement years.

It *can* be daunting to think about having enough money for retirement. Discouraging even. Company pensions are becoming an endangered species. We're told that the Social Security system will go bankrupt in twenty-plus years; should we count on it at all? As for personal savings, it's tough to make it through the month, let alone save for twenty years from now. How can we be sure we'll have enough when the Big Transition comes? And how can we be sure our savings will last as long as we do?

Most likely you picked up this book because you're contemplating these questions too. We're going to address them together, you and I. We'll cut through the jungle of information, choose the paths that are best for you, and put you on the road to a financially secure future.

I think you're going to enjoy the process.

❑ We will take an exciting look at what financial freedom can mean to you when retirement time comes.

❑ We'll look ahead into your not-so-distant future to determine how much money you're likely to need and the factors that may be working against you. *But we'll also underscore the factors working in your favor.*

❑ We will help you determine how much you should be saving and investing *now* to realistically provide for your retirement years . . .

❑ . . . and help you find more money *now* to save and invest for your future (hundreds, possibly thousands, of dollars you didn't realize you had).

❑ But we'll invest the bulk of our time together exploring seven key commitments that will help you *make the most of what you've got* and build solid financial strength for the coming years. With these in place, you'll be able to approach your retirement with confidence, peace of mind, and the financial freedom to pursue your dreams.

THE SEVEN PILLARS OF FINANCIALLY INDEPENDENT RETIREMENT

To help you envision the type of financial freedom we're talking about, we'll use a visual metaphor. As you gaze ahead to your retirement years, imagine a round, monument-type structure complete with foundation, seven supporting pillars (six around the perimeter, one in the center), and a roof. The edifice, strong, solid, and secure, represents the financial strength you hope to enjoy when the big day comes.

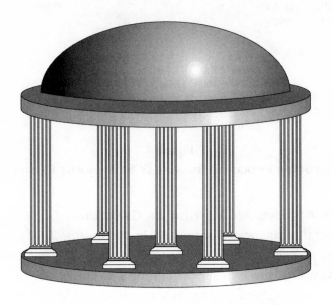

Figure 1.1
FINANCIAL STRENGTH FOR THE NEW RETIREMENT

Figure 1.1 provides a side view. You don't see all seven pillars from this vantage point, but you do see a strong, sound structure. Its roof represents one of the chief benefits of all the pillars working together: *financial peace of mind.*

Figure 1.2, a top view, shows the strategic placement of our seven pillars. At the center is our most crucial support column, placed there to underscore its higher level of importance and its role in helping the other six do their jobs well. Surrounding it are six columns positioned in a circle, each working in combination with the others to strengthen and support the building.

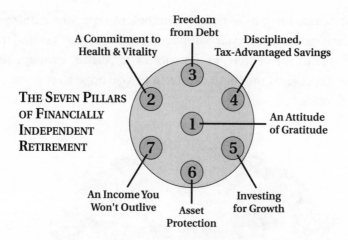

Figure 1.2
THE SEVEN PILLARS OF FINANCIALLY INDEPENDENT RETIREMENT

THE FIRST PILLAR: AN ATTITUDE OF GRATITUDE

Central to financial freedom is a heartfelt *attitude of gratitude*—a sincere spirit of thankfulness to God for every big and small blessing in your life. From this heart of gratitude comes the natural, joyful overflow of sharing with your community, church, and worthwhile endeavors around the world.

THE SECOND PILLAR: A COMMITMENT TO HEALTH AND VITALITY

Our second pillar is *a commitment to health and vitality*—knowing that good health is vital (a) to help avoid big medical expenses down the road and (b) to the fitness, energy, and vitality you will want in order to truly enjoy an active, fulfilling life style.

THE THIRD PILLAR: FREEDOM FROM DEBT

Next comes *freedom from debt*—breaking and staying free of those Buy Now, Pay Forever habits that rob your future as you pay for your past. We'll help you break free of consumer debt for good, liberating thousands of dollars that you can set aside for your future. We'll also help you make sure that, when retirement time comes, you'll be free of consumer debt and able to turn all those debt-servicing dollars into YOU-servicing dollars.

THE FOURTH PILLAR: DISCIPLINED, TAX-ADVANTAGED SAVINGS

As your consumer-debt load lightens, you'll be able to direct even more dollars toward savings for the future. Which brings us to our fourth pillar: *disciplined, tax-advantaged savings.* Some of that money will go toward a contingency reserve of three to six months' living expenses to help handle life's surprises. Your major savings commitment, however, is for the long term, because here you enjoy the "turbocharged" growing power of tax-advantaged savings that allow you to tax-deduct your contributions and defer taxes on earnings.

THE FIFTH PILLAR: INVESTING FOR GROWTH

Our fifth pillar is *investing for growth. Saving* is the simple act of setting money aside; *investing* is putting those savings to work to grow over time. Even the most diligent savers will short-sheet themselves if they leave all their funds in "safe" places such as bank accounts, money market funds, certificates of deposit, and Treasury bills. For long-term retirement savings, you will want to put your money to work more aggressively. We'll examine the rules for investment success, then set you up with some simple, powerful strategies to help your money grow at annual averages of 10 to 12 percent or better. You may be pleasantly surprised at the potential!

THE SIXTH PILLAR: ASSET PROTECTION

Next comes the important pillar called *asset protection,* "safety nets" to guard against losing what you're working so hard to build. We'll underscore the types of insurance coverage you shouldn't be without . . . and several that are a waste of your money.

THE SEVENTH PILLAR: AN INCOME YOU WON'T OUTLIVE

Our last pillar, *an income you won't outlive,* addresses one of today's most prevalent fears among retirees, pre-retirees, and baby boomers alike: *"Will I outlive my resources? Will I have to move in with my children or depend on the government?"* While it's important that adult children welcome parents-in-need with open arms, the truth is that most of us really wouldn't want to move in with our adult children (unless, of course, we have a mean streak). Moving in would not only feel like a loss of our independence, but it would also impose hardships on our kids' budgets and life styles as they seek to raise their own families. We also know that having our finances expire before we do means subsisting rather than thriving, and we want to *thrive!* Thus, our seventh pillar calls for converting our assets into a series of reliable income streams. Combined with savvy spending choices, these help ensure that we will have all the money we need for as long as we will need it.

With all seven pillars in place, you can indeed enjoy financial independence in your retirement years—freedom to live the kind of life you want to live, with financial peace of mind. While it's true that it's better to start early, there is always time to greatly improve your financial future whether you're a young adult, midlifer, or pre-retiree. The key is to begin *now* to put the "pillars" in place. Together, we're going to do just that.

RETHINKING "RETIREMENT"

But we're not focusing on personal finance simply to help you accumulate wealth. Money is only an *implement* of life, not life itself. It's a means, not an end. But the truth is that you live in a world in which your financial condition is likely to be the chief determinant of the type of life you're able to enjoy when the Big Transition comes. Your finances will determine how free you will be to *retire the way you want to and when you want to.* A healthy financial picture will empower you to *keep all your options open,* free to travel, work part-time, volunteer, go back to school, recreate, or pursue a lifelong dream.

So our goal goes beyond making the most of what you have for a secure financial future. Dig a little deeper into your psyche, probe beneath the financial questions, and I think you'll make an interesting discovery. Most of our retirement-oriented concerns actually could be summed up in one deeper, more basic question:

"How can I make the most of the rest of my life?"

That's the foundational question we're dealing with here. Retirement planning doesn't end with financial planning. Retirement planning also involves evaluating your attitudes, perhaps even rethinking your philosophy of retirement. After all, if you're going to spend up to one-third of your life there—and if you're wanting to build the financial resources you'll need for those years—doesn't it follow that you should also plan on making those years some of the best, most productive times of your life?

You see, I want to encourage you to blow the traditional view of retirement out of the water—to ignite a spark of fresh, creative thinking about your laterlife. I'm encouraging my generation to think far beyond the RV, the rocking chair, and the pursuit of the Small White Ball when defining life's purpose in retirement.

This is why I've titled our visit together *Never Retire*. Sure, we may all leave our jobs or careers someday (many of us have little choice in the matter). But I hope, after investing some time with me, you will resolve to "never retire" as most men and women have retired in the past. I hope you'll regard "retirement" not as your time to sit on the sidelines, but as your time to *step up to the plate* for bigger and better things.

Kathy and I prefer to think of the last two or three decades of our lives not as the time to sit back, but as the time to step up. We may indeed "retire" from our present professions—and we probably will hike more trails, see more sights, and enjoy our own pursuit of the Small White Ball. But, God willing, we also hope to use the time and resources of those years in ways that are both a blast for us and a blessing for our world. Instead of the cessation of productivity, retirement is going to provide a fresh start.

A fresh start . . .

Hmmmm.

What if we *were* to rethink retirement? To look upon it as . . . *Commencement*?

Commencement. A fresh start.

The time of new beginnings.

A new attitude.

Looking forward, not back.

Seizing the day. Seizing the *decades*.

Commencement. It's truly the first day of the rest of our lives. The start of the "New Retirement." A take-charge, proactive time. Always discovering. Always learning. Joyful, vital, productive. Not self-absorbed, but others-oriented—and thus self-actualizing.

It's not a time to retreat; it's a time to *rejuvenate*. Not a time to grow old, but a time to *grow*. Not a time to give in, but a time to *give back*.

In this spirit of Commencement, your retirement—your *New Retirement*—can actually bring about a personal rebirth. You'll enjoy a rejuvenation of your outlook, a quickening of your step, and a strengthening of your spirit as you approach each day with joyful expectancy. (Kind of energizes you already, doesn't it?)

Isn't this the kind of life you'd *really* like to live when "retirement time" comes?

I thought so.

It's the twofold purpose of our visit together in these pages. We're not building financial freedom in order to live as prisoners of the old retirement. We're building financial independence to help transform the prospect of retirement into the promise of Commencement—the time of new beginnings, the start of New Retirement. We're seeking to

Make the most of what you've got . . . to make the most of the rest of your life.

If this is a goal you can get excited about, turn the page with me and we'll get started.

THE NEVER RETIRE GLOSSARY

◇ **Baby boomers:** The men and women born between 1946 and 1964. When World War II ended in 1945, millions of GIs returned home ready to make up for lost time. In 1964 they finally collapsed, exhausted, to enjoy the pitter-patter of 76 million boomers running around their households.

◇ **Commencement:** The new perspective we're going to adopt as we rethink retirement. It regards our Big Transition not as the time to cease and desist, but as the time of new beginnings. Instead of Retirement Day, we'll look on it as Commencement Day.

◇ **Financial independence:** If you want to become filthy rich overnight, while you sleep, this isn't the book for you. (There are, however, dozens of late-night infomercials ready to take your cash.) When we talk financial independence, we mean building the financial resources that will allow you to enjoy the freedom to truly *live* the rest of your life when your paychecks cease—free to take full advantage of the many opportunities you will have. We'll also refer to this as *financial freedom*.

◇ **Laterlife:** I'm not going to use terms like "old age." And since we're rethinking retirement, I'll even try to avoid "senior citizen" as much as I can. Instead, I'm going to coin terms such as "laterlife" and "seniority" to refer to the period of life traditionally known as the "retirement years." *Laterlifers* are those who have made the shift from full-time career to retirement mode—hopefully, to Commencement and New Retirement.

◇ **Midlife** has little to do with emotional crises. No need, men, to go out and reclaim your youth with a red Porsche. For purposes of retirement planning, we'll use this term to refer to the period of life between ages thirty-five and sixty. *Midlifers* are people in this age range. Many midlifers indeed face a *financial* crisis, but a Porsche isn't the answer. (It may have been part of the problem.)

◇ **New Retirement:** The upbeat life style and attitudes you'll enjoy when you regard retirement as Commencement—the time of new beginnings. Instead of a time to step down, it's a time to step up. Instead of a time to rust out, it's a time to reach out—and *make the most of the rest of your life.*

◇ **Pre-retirees:** Men and women within ten years of retirement from their jobs or professions.

◇ **Retirement:** The act of leaving the full-time working life (we'll also refer to it as *the Big Transition* and *Commencement Day*) to live out one's laterlife in a more leisurely fashion; also used to refer to the years following one's working life, which society readily associates with hammocks, tee times, Winnebagos, and Early Bird Specials. All of these pursuits are fine, but laterlife can and should be so much richer. We're going to reshape the concept into *New Retirement*—a perspective and life style that'll keep our adrenaline flowing and give us good reasons to get up each morning.

◇ ***Retirement age:*** Traditionally age sixty-five, but only because the creators of Social Security in the 1930s designated this as the age one qualifies for the Social Security pension. Seemed like a safe choice at the time, for the average life span then was sixty-three. But instead of letting our government or employer tell us when we should retire, we're going to take charge . . . and redefine retirement age as "any age we want it to be."

PART ONE

GOOD
QUESTIONS

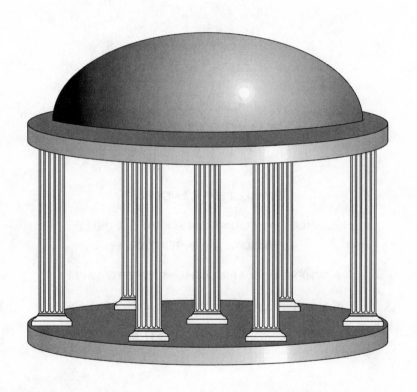

TWO

WILL I HAVE ENOUGH?

How much will you need to save for New Retirement?

According to the U.S. Census Bureau, almost half of all Americans over age sixty-five have a household income below $15,000 a year. Only 18 percent have annual incomes of more than $35,000. These figures include Social Security benefits.

It's numbers such as these that have startled many pre-retirees and baby boomers into reality about their own futures. Take Patrick and Jan, both in their late forties.

"When we see the numbers, how so many retirees struggle to get by, we start to get nervous," Patrick admits. "We're fifteen, sixteen years away from retiring, and we don't want to experience that if we can help it."

"We know we need to be saving more and planning better," Jan adds. "Patrick's been putting some aside in the retirement plan at work, but we need to do more."

"No problem," Patrick says. "We'll just live off the kids."

Jan's brow furrows.

"Just kidding," Patrick grins. "Seriously, we are concerned. And confused. How do we know how much we'll need for retirement? You know, so we can enjoy ourselves . . ."

" . . . and so we don't run out of money after five or ten years," Jan adds.

GOOD QUESTIONS

Whether you're ten, twenty, or thirty years from retirement age, the questions Patrick and Jan are asking may be on your mind as well. If you're like most midlifers, up to this point the bulk of your annual earnings has gone to paying the mortgage or rent, groceries, bills, and car payments. You're also paying out hundreds, maybe more, to service credit card debt. You may be contributing to your church or favorite charity. And with all this going on, you're trying to tuck away some savings for big future expenses: rainy days, college for the kids, retirement for you.

Like Patrick and Jan, you may feel that, under the circumstances, you're doing the best you can for the long term. But is it enough? To paraphrase Patrick's question: *How will you know you're in sound fiscal shape as you approach Commencement Day?* And paraphrasing Jan: *. . . so that you won't run out of money before you run out of living to do?*

Good questions.

You've heard the adage "Aim at nothing and you're bound to hit it." It underscores the importance of specificity, of a tangible, measurable goal that enables you to assess your progress and helps ensure that you'll be where you need to be when a deadline nears.

Financial planners often come across singles and couples who need to be asking the good questions. When clients are asked about retirement goals, a typical response goes something like this: "I'd like to retire someday and have lots of money so I can have lots of fun."

To which a wise planner replies, "Please define what you mean by *someday*. Define *lots of money*. Define *lots of fun*."

Until you get specific, until you put things in tangible, measurable terms, there's no way to know what you will need and how you can get there. No way to measure progress. It's a timeless principle, just as true today as it was two thousand years ago when Jesus Christ said, "Suppose one of you wants to build a tower. Will he not first sit down and estimate the cost to see if he has enough money to complete it?"(Luke 14:28).

Aim at nothing and you're bound to hit . . . nothing.

So the questions Patrick, Jan, you, and I ask are *good questions.* They call for specificity. They will not only help us gain a reasonable idea of where we're likely to stand as we move to New Retirement, but they will also help us see what kinds of midcourse corrections may be necessary along the way.

HOW MUCH ANNUAL INCOME WILL YOU NEED?

Our first step is to try to estimate the amount of annual income we will need when Commencement Day arrives. Doing so is an imprecise science, to be sure, because much can change between now and then. And I'm going to steer you clear of lengthy line-item worksheets on which you guess what each of your monthly expenses will be when you make the Big Transition. While such worksheets are helpful, they can also be intimidating—they look like hard work, so they get put off. Thus, few readers will actually complete these multipage worksheets until they're within a year or two of saying good-bye to their paychecks.

Fortunately, for the numerically challenged and anyone else who hates lengthy accounting procedures, there's a quicker, simpler method for estimating your retirement-income needs.

Financial experts predict that our retirement needs will be anywhere between 60 and 90 percent of our present living expenses. Thus, if your monthly expenses presently total $2,500, you'll probably require $1,500 to $2,250 a month in your retirement years. Why will your expenses be less? Because, the reasoning goes, you will no longer incur job-related costs such as transportation, office attire, childcare, and daily lunches. You may also have paid off your mortgage, freed yourself of other debts, and given your kids a loving but resolute push from the nest.

But 60 to 90 percent isn't very precise, is it? Kind of like a weathercaster saying, "It's going to be bright and sunny all day tomorrow if it doesn't rain." I also don't think this range is appropriate for everyone, because we're all approaching seniority from different perspectives, with different life styles in mind. To sharpen the picture, we really need to know several personal factors about you. For instance . . .

❏ *At what age would you like Commencement to take place?* Don't target age sixty-five just because it's what society says; when would *you* like to make the transition? For what it's worth, if you were born prior to 1943, the age for a full Social Security retirement pension is sixty-five; if you were born between 1943 and 1959, it's age sixty-six. For those born in 1960 or later, the age is sixty-seven. But what does your heart tell you? There's no good reason to voluntarily leave your chosen field until you sense in your heart that it's time. The older you are upon entering New Retirement, the fewer years you'll need to self-fund from your nest egg. You'll also have more built up because the added time at work will enable you to make more contributions and watch them compound.

❏ *What big obligations will you have then?* Will your house be paid off, or will you be making mortgage or rent payments? Will your kids be out of the nest, through college, and on their own, or have you made promises to them that may obligate you into seniority? Will you be caring for aged parents? Make your best prediction based on your circumstances; any of these factors will increase your income needs.

❏ *What kind of life style do you want to live?* Do you want to stay put or move to another part of the country? Do you desire a quiet life, staying mostly around home and yard? Or would you like to hit the road and visit places you've always wanted to see? Want to do some volunteer work in town? go back to school? self-finance a short-term mission trip overseas? Your desired life style has a big say in determining the income you'll need each month.

❏ *Do you want to continue working?* at least part-time? seasonally? Many retirees find that, after the first euphoric weeks of retirement, they're restless and bored—ready to go back to some kind of work. Let's face it, God created us to be productive. Contrary to modern misconsensus, work was not part of the curse God placed on Adam and Eve for their disobedience in the Garden of Eden, for the Bible tells us that Adam worked the garden with delight *prior to* their sin (Genesis 2:15). God's plan is for us to work and to find joy in it, because he created us with hearts for productivity. In fact, we will not find society's modern concept of "retirement" mentioned in the Bible or throughout history, for that matter.* As people aged, they remained productive; when they could no longer do physical labor, they were still valued for their wisdom, leadership qualities, and street smarts.

Perhaps this helps explain studies revealing that, when men or women suddenly cease working, in many cases their health and attitudes deteriorate dramatically. Whether we initiate retirement or our company does, the sudden drop in productivity from forty hours to zero really can feel like being put out to pasture. Continuing work in some capacity will not only stretch and strengthen your financial reserves, it will also help keep you physically and mentally healthy as you stay in touch with people, daily challenges, and job skills.

❏ *What is your life expectancy?* Thanks to modern medicine and preventive care, life spans have grown steadily over the years. What's your family history in this area? If your parents and grandparents were active into their eighties and nineties, and if you're in good health yourself, you may live three decades or more after you quit full-time work. It's important to be conservative here; you don't want to draw down your reserves too fast. Even though insurance actuarial tables may put you six feet under in your late seventies or

---

*Retirement as we know it did not become a reality until the 1930s, when our government was seeking a way to motivate older workers to move along and make way for the huge influx of younger workers in need of jobs during and after the Great Depression. Social Security was launched to help encourage such a move.

mid-eighties, thumb your nose at them and plan on living well into your nineties.

PROJECTING YOUR INCOME NEEDS

With these factors in mind, we're going to modify the 60 to 90 percent range that planners have traditionally proposed for retirement-income planning. We'll keep the projections simple (your hand-held calculator will do), add some specifics to better serve *you,* and in just ten minutes or so you'll have a good idea of (1) the annual income you will need when Commencement Day arrives and (2) the "Big Sum" you'll need to save up between now and then from which to draw that annual income.

❑ First, let's cross the 60 percent projection off our list right away, unless you long to hole up in a tent and live on dandelion greens. Most of us would require a drastic life style change if we suddenly incurred a 40 percent cut in income. We want to thrive, not merely survive.

❑ Let's also not limit our projection to 90 percent of current expenses. If you dream of stopping work and spending some big bucks to travel, purchase a new home, volunteer, return to class, or climb Everest, you may in fact need more than your present level of expenses. You may want to plan on 120 percent, at least during the first decade of New Retirement when you're likely to be most active.

❑ Add up all your present monthly expenses: $_____.

❑ Subtract from this amount major expenses you probably won't face once you've entered retirement: contributions to retirement plans, children's college costs, mortgage payments (if you're on course to pay off your house), credit card debt payments, etc. Result: $_____.

❑ Multiply the result by 12: $_____.

❑ Add all your quarterly, semiannual, or annual expenses such as insurance premiums, association fees, property taxes, and Christmas expenses.

❑ Total Annual Expenses: $_____.

❑ Multiply your Total Annual Expenses by

- 75 to 80 percent if
  - your mortgage will be paid off,
  - all other debt will be paid off, and
  - you foresee a relatively modest, home-based life style.

- 80 to 100 percent if
  - your mortgage will be mostly paid off,
  - all other debt will be paid off, and
  - you foresee continuing your present life style.

- 100 to 120 percent if
  - you'll be taking on a new mortgage of any size or
  - you don't think you'll have other debt fully paid off or
  - you foresee an adventurous, higher-expense life style.

Percentage selected: _____%

Total Projected Annual Expenses: $_____.

❑ Aha! Thought I'd forget about income taxes, didn't you? Well, I wish I could, but our dear Uncle Sam also has something to say about it and he's bigger than I am. Assuming most of your retirement saving was accomplished via tax-deductible, tax-deferred vehicles such as 401(k)s or IRAs, you will indeed need to pay income tax as you draw funds from these accounts. (Exception: the Roth IRA. More on that later.)

Unfortunately, Congress doesn't make long-term tax planning easy because it is always tinkering with the tax system. The best you can do is plan in today's terms, then make adjustments as both congresspersons and time pass. It's wise to play it conservatively here too—so we're going to use today's marginal tax rates to estimate what your federal income tax may be. (You pay a lower rate on your *first* dollars of annual income and progressively more as your taxable income edges into higher tax brackets. Your *marginal rate* is the rate you pay on your *last* dollars of income each year. Thus, by using your marginal rate, you'll be estimating on the high side and possibly building a bit of "cushion" into your projection.) Here goes:

Take the Total Projected Annual Expenses from above and multiply it by your present federal marginal tax bracket:

FEDERAL TAX BRACKET	SINGLE	MARRIED FILING JOINTLY
15%	Less than $25,750	Less than $43,050
28%	$25,750 to $62,450	$43,050 to $104,050
31%	$62,450 to $130,250	$104,050 to $158,550
36%	$130,250 to $283,150	$158,550 to $283,150
39.6%	More than $283,150	More than $283,150

Figure 2.1

YOUR FEDERAL MARGINAL TAX BRACKET

For tax year 1999—destined for change thereafter as Congress continues tinkering. See the most recent federal tax preparation guide when updating your personal projections.

Projected Annual Federal Tax: $_____.

❑ Estimate your *state tax* in the same way. You can do so by looking in your most recent state income tax preparation booklet or by calling your state's department of revenue.

Projected Annual State Tax: $_____.

❑ Add your Projected Annual Federal and State Taxes to your Total Projected Annual Expenses. The result is the total annual income you're likely to need upon retirement.

> ## ANNUAL RETIREMENT INCOME NEEDED: $_____.

For simplicity's sake, these projections are in today's dollars and at today's rates, based on what you know at this moment. To account for inflation or tax-code changes, you'll want to review and adjust projected expenses and income needs annually between now and Commencement Day.

HOW MUCH SAVINGS WILL YOU NEED TO DRAW THAT INCOME?

Now that you have a good idea of your annual retirement-income needs, we come to the Big Sum—the total amount you'll need to have saved by Commencement Day in order to meet your projected annual expenses. We'll be conservative here as well, since I suspect you'd rather not run out of money fifteen years before you pass on. Let's assume the following:

(1) During the first five or ten years of New Retirement, you will try to keep investment principal intact and rely only on investment earnings for income.

(2) In the first five or ten years of retirement you will seek to earn 8 percent or better average annual return.

(3) As you grow older, you may gradually invest more conservatively—say, for 6 percent return—and can begin drawing from principal as future projections allow.

The equation we'll use for calculating the total amount you'll need upon retirement is a simple one:

$ (annual income needed) divided by .08 (8 percent) =
$ (total Big Sum needed)

❑ Take your calculator and punch in the Annual Retirement Income Needed you calculated above. Divide by .08. The result is the minimum total amount you'll need to have invested at 8 percent in order to draw your desired annual "salary" in laterlife.

Want a quick example? Let's say your annual income needed, including taxes, came to $50,000. Enter $50,000 into your calculator. Divide $50,000 by .08.

The resulting number is $625,000. (Eight percent of this amount is $50,000.) If you average an 8 percent or better return on investment and don't invade your principal, your retirement funds could continue to spin off $50,000 per year indefinitely, leaving your $625,000 essentially intact. And the day will come when you can begin drawing from your principal as well.

Six hundred twenty-five thousand dollars, then, is the Big Sum for this example—the minimum total amount you should aim to have in retirement savings before Commencement. More than that will give you even more breathing room for cost-of-living increases or new opportunities that may come your way.

Now plug in your own numbers. What's *your* Big Sum?

TOTAL AMOUNT NEEDED ON COMMENCEMENT DAY: $_____.

Again, projections are in today's dollars and should be reviewed and adjusted annually to account for inflation or changing circumstances.

TAKE THREE DEEP BREATHS . . .

Now I realize that such numbers as your Big Sum may not be suitable for impressionable readers. If talk of half-million-dollar nest eggs threatens to bring on an aneurysm, sit down, take three deep breaths, and squeeze my hand. You may be wondering, as the room spins before your eyes, how you can possibly accumulate the Big Sum necessary to provide the annual retirement income you'll need.

Granted, your required nest egg *is* a lot of money. And almost all of us are in the same boat, which is why we need to take financial planning seriously. And why you and I are visiting together over the next several days.

But please don't feel intimidated or discouraged. Your Big Sum may or may not appear reachable to you right now, but we're going to demonstrate how you *can* make that number a reality—or adapt and adjust your planning so you can still have all the money you need when the Big Transition takes place.

Always keep in mind our big picture: We're not talking numbers just for the sake of numbers. Our goal is to be financially free from dependence on the government, our children, and charity—financially *independent* to pursue the dreams of the New Retirement. We're seeking to *make the most of what we've got . . . to make the most of the rest of our lives.*

So now you know what you're aiming for—which means your chances of success are dramatically improved already! In the next four chapters we'll demonstrate how your goal is indeed reachable—how you may already have more going for you than you think. Then in Part Two we'll get specific with seven balanced strategies to help you build the financial independence we've been talking about.

ACTION POINTS

Throughout *Never Retire* we've provided Action Points pages to help you personalize and apply what you're reading. Use these pages to record key steps you feel led to take in preparation for New Retirement.

HABITS I WANT TO CHANGE

-
-
-
-

NEW ATTITUDES I WANT TO LIVE BY

-
-
-
-

ACTION STEPS I NEED TO TAKE

1.
2.
3.
4.
5.

THREE

SHOULD I COUNT ON SOCIAL SECURITY? A PENSION? AN INHERITANCE?

*What you should know before planning on
these sources of retirement income.*

After seeing the Big Sum we'll need to build by Commencement Day, it's quite natural to wonder what kind of "outside" funds may be available during New Retirement to supplement our own personal savings. Traditionally, these outside income sources include (1) the Social Security system, (2) corporate-paid pensions, and (3) possible financial inheritances.

But should we count on Social Security? (If so, how much?) And how should we factor a corporate pension or a potential inheritance into our financial planning?

SHOULD YOU COUNT ON SOCIAL SECURITY?

Historically, one of the first places retirees and pre-retirees have looked for financial assurance is our nation's Social Security system. The program was born in 1935 as one of FDR's initiatives to bring the country out of the Great Depression. Its purpose was to provide a safety-net incentive for workers to leave the labor pool at age sixty-five, which then would create openings for the droves of younger adults in urgent need of jobs.

It was a relatively safe move at the time, since the average life expectancy in 1935 was sixty-three. And during Social Security's first decade, more than forty workers contributed to the system for every one retiree drawing a stipend. The maximum annual contribution was $30.

How times have changed! Today life spans have increased to the point that a typical retiree may draw benefits for fifteen to thirty years instead of just four or five. Today there are only three workers supporting every retiree, and the Social Security board of trustees projects that by the year 2025 the ratio could be as low as two workers per beneficiary. Social Security taxes have increased, but so have payouts as the senior population grows larger and Congress indexes benefits to inflation. In addition, benefits have been expanded to include health and disability insurance.

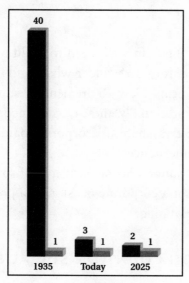

Figure 3.1

NUMBER OF WORKERS SUPPORTING

EACH SOCIAL SECURITY RECIPIENT

As a result, for the past several years we've been hearing that the Social Security system could actually be bankrupt in the 2020s unless drastic measures are taken. Most trend watchers do not feel Congress or presidents will allow the system to go bankrupt—the senior political lobby is already a powerful one and will be exponentially strengthened as baby boomers begin joining its ranks in a few years. Expect politicians to keep the system solvent by continuing to increase taxes, delaying and reducing benefits, and instituting some form of privatization. The heat of this political hot potato will only increase as 76 million of us join the senior voting bloc.

FULL SOCIAL SECURITY BENEFITS: WHEN WILL YOU QUALIFY?

Because of increasing life spans and greater demands on the system, Congress has already tweaked the qualifying ages for future Social Security recipients. Those born prior to 1943 continue to qualify for full pensions at age sixty-five. If you were born between 1943 and 1959, your eligibility age is sixty-six. If you were born in 1960 or later, you'll wait until you're at least sixty-seven, and don't be surprised by further extensions of the qualifying age up to age seventy. Stay tuned; this is Congress we're talking about.

Meanwhile, as politicians wrangle, there is much debate over whether future retirees can count on help from the Social Security system at all. Baby boomers have been doubtful, to put it kindly. Younger workers are even more skeptical about the system's viability. I recall one survey reporting that more men and women under the age of thirty-four believe in UFOs than believe they'll receive Social Security benefits.

So how should you plan regarding Social Security? First and foremost, it's crucial to recognize that Social Security was never meant to provide one's entire retirement income. It was established as *a supplement, a safety net,* and continues to pay only about one-fourth of most people's monthly income needs.

Most financial observers feel that, while adjustments are inevitable, the basic system is solvent enough for today's pre-retirees and baby boomers to plan on *some* form of Social Security income supplement. If you were to enter New Retirement today, you would receive approximately $12,000 per year per working person (today's dollars)—half that for a spouse who hasn't accrued sufficient Social Security credits. If you want to count on Social Security income at all, cap your projections at the following figures:

Figure 3.2

ESTIMATED SOCIAL SECURITY PENSION INCOME

(TODAY'S DOLLARS)

QUALIFIED RECIPIENTS	ESTIMATED ANNUAL PENSION	50% OF ESTIMATED PENSION
1 working person	$12,000	$6,000
Plus 1 nonworking spouse	$18,000	$9,000
2 working persons	$24,000	$12,000

The encouraging part of all this is that any income we do receive from the system can reduce the required size of our Big Sum as well as our annual draw from it. But since the system is shaky and, worse, is in the hands of politicians, I suggest we plan on only 50 percent or less of today's payout levels. Many financial planners recommend planning on no Social Security income at all.

WILL YOU RECEIVE A CORPORATE PENSION?

Until recent years, the typical corporate pension was the defined-benefit package. The company funded it for you, took responsibility for managing its underlying investments, and, upon vesting, guaranteed you a specific monthly pension upon your retirement.

But like nearly everything else, this has changed. The old pensions assumed two-way corporate loyalty and long tenures, but those qualities have now become rare. Downsizings, buyouts, and new technologies have made corporations less loyal to employees, while the constant quest for upward mobility has prompted baby boomers to change companies more frequently. Either way, if termination happens before the employee is fully vested, he will receive only the vested amount. If the company should go belly up, its pension fund may fold with it. Thus, defined-benefit pensions are becoming either dinosaurs or difficult to count on.

In most companies the dinosaur has been replaced by the 401(k), to which the *employee,* not the employer, is responsible for making contributions (although the employer may match a portion of the employee's contribution). The employee is also responsible for managing the program's underlying investments. It's a win-win situation, really: less responsibility (and liability) for the employer, more control for the employee. If you change jobs, your 401(k) can go with you.

In Part Two we'll see why the 401(k) has been aptly called "the best investment in the world." For now, I just want to touch on the point that the relative security of the traditional corporate pension is quickly vanishing from the scene. If you have worked someplace with a defined-benefit package and are entitled to a pension, check with the company's human resources staff for an estimate of your annual pension income. If, to your knowledge, the fiscal health of the company is sound, you can subtract the annual amount of your defined-benefit pension from your calculation of your Annual Retirement Income Required. However, most of us will have little or no defined-benefit income to plan on.

WHAT ABOUT AN INHERITANCE?

Our folks timed it well. They are not only full beneficiaries of the Social Security system (perhaps the last generation to be so), they also are beneficiaries of an unprecedented real estate boom that enabled them to buy houses after World War II for $20,000 and sell them upon retirement for $160,000. Blend those phenomena with their solid work ethic, frugal life styles, disciplined savings, and a stock market that's risen fifteenfold in thirty years, and our parents' generation has built a huge asset base—much of which will be passed on to their adult children. That's *us*. In what will be the largest transfer of wealth in American history, retirees are expected to hand down some $10.4 trillion over the next twenty to thirty years.

As we know, not all of our parents participated equally in the economic boom. Neither will all of us share equally in the future transfer of wealth. Adult children who do receive some inheritance (and invest it wisely) may quickly account for a good portion of the Big Sum they'll need on their own Commencement Day. It's difficult, though, to factor inheritances into long-range planning because we simply may not know our parents' fiscal situation, it's awkward to ask, they may not want to tell, and no one knows for sure how much of their asset base will remain once they are gone.

WHOSE MONEY? (A HEART-TO-HEART ON INHERITANCES)

I carry a deep conviction that, in our long-range planning, we should not count on or even make broad hints about inheritances from our parents. Remember that an inheritance is a *gift,* not an obligation. Our moms and dads have already worked thousands of hours and spent tens of thousands to raise us. What they have now is what they also labored hard to build for their own laterlives.

Yet many today seem to regard inheritance as an entitlement. I have personally witnessed disgusting examples in which senior parents decided to use some of their hard-earned reserves for a special trip or fun purchase—while their presumptuous, boomer-age children sputtered, "Mom and Dad are spending *our* money."

Whose money?

A few years ago, after my dad went to be with the Lord, Mom mentioned to Kathy and me, "I'd really like to have money left to pass along to my kids when *I'm* gone." While we deeply appreciate Mom's sentiment, we never want our parents to feel any kind of pressure or obligation in this area.

"Mom," I replied, "I've already received my inheritance—it's the love and upbringing you and Dad gave me growing up. That's priceless and it's forever. Your money is *yours.* We want you to use it to make the most of your life."

That's truly the way Kathy and I feel. If we should receive something from our parents someday, we will of course be grateful. But we would look upon any such bequest as *an unexpected gift, not an entitlement.* It's certainly not an obligation on their part, for our parents have already given us far more than money, far more than we deserve, far more than we can ever repay.

With my mother, I summed it up this way: "Mom, we hope you spend your last dollar on your last day before going to heaven." In other words, what you have is yours, not ours. Use it to fill your days with gladness. Mom chuckled at that, and I think she was relieved. I hope so.

If you've ever caught yourself mentally counting a potential inheritance from your parents, I hope these words encourage you to examine your heart. It's not *your* inheritance. Not your money. It's fully, completely theirs. Encourage them to make the most of the rest of *their* lives. They deserve it.

If you do end up receiving an inheritance, I hope you will look upon it not as an entitlement, but as an unexpected gift. I hope you will honor your parents' lives by sharing a good portion of any inheritance with worthy causes and ministries you believe in, then using the rest to get clear of debt and invest for your own future.

If, on the other hand, your parents are unable to leave financial help behind, remember that such things are not to be expected anyway. Rejoice in all the good things they've left you—the deeper legacy of nurture, character, faith in God, a good name. A financial inheritance only pales in comparison.

IF IT'S TO BE . . .

As we've considered Social Security, corporate pensions, and inheritances, you may have found some tangible possibilities for helping supplement your annual income in laterlife. But I also want to show that all three "outside" sources are uncertain; none is a done deal. You may or may not receive help from Uncle Sam. You may or may not receive any type of defined-benefit corporate pension. You may or may not receive an inheritance. You will want to be conservative when planning for any of these three income sources, if you choose to plan on them at all.

Well, then. If we can't rely on Social Security or a corporate-paid pension or a big inheritance, what *do* we rely on? How do we build the financial reserves we know we will need when we are on our own? There is an old motivational saying that seems appropriate here:

If it's to be, it's up to me.

That's the bottom line: It comes down to what *you* do to prepare, not what others do for you. It depends on how diligently you set funds aside and how aggressively you put those funds to work. On how wisely you harness the power of tax deferral and compounding. On how you utilize the Seven Pillars of Financially Independent Retirement to achieve financial readiness for the pursuit of your New Retirement dreams.

No one else is going to do it for you.

It's up to you.

The truth about our responsibility to prepare for the future was set down three thousand years ago by Solomon, whose legendary wisdom applies to our generation as much as it did his own:

A wise man thinks ahead; a fool doesn't, and even brags about it!
. . . The wise man saves for the future, but the foolish man spends whatever he gets. (Proverbs 13:16; 21:20, TLB)

By now you may be thinking, *OK, I realize that a financially independent retirement is up to me. That I need to save consistently in order to make it happen. But I have bills to pay—lots of them. Where do I find extra money to save and invest for the future?*

Believe me, I understand. Sometimes the challenge seems overwhelming. It takes lots of money to keep up with present expenses, let alone set money aside for the future. But there's help.

An encouraging word. A key, reassuring principle of personal finance:

You have more money than you think.

Personalize that statement and repeat it to yourself: _I have more money than I think._ Let it sink in. It's not just wishful thinking; in fact, I'm willing to go out on a limb and state that it's a reality. You have more money than you think you do, and with a few smart moves you can pull it from limbo and put it to work to grow toward your Commencement Day.

You'll find it in the next chapter. Hang on to your hat.

ACTION POINTS

Throughout *Never Retire* we've provided Action Points pages to help you personalize and apply what you're reading. Use these pages to record key steps you feel led to take in preparation for New Retirement.

HABITS I WANT TO CHANGE

-
-
-
-

NEW ATTITUDES I WANT TO LIVE BY

-
-
-
-

ACTION STEPS I NEED TO TAKE

1.
2.
3.
4.
5.

FOUR

WHERE WILL I FIND THE MONEY TO SAVE?

Twelve places to find money you can set aside for your future.

"A re you kidding me?" Patrick is smiling—a forced smile, per-haps—but you can see incredulity in his eyes. Jan's eyes are glazed, but she twitters a nervous laugh. They have just learned that in order to draw $50,000 annual income in retirement, they will need a nest egg of $625,000 averaging 8 percent annual return. To draw $60,000, they'll need $750,000. And to draw $75,000, which is close to their present combined income, they will need a Big Sum of $938,000.

Numbers like these are totally foreign to their frame of refer-ence. And at age forty-nine, they have just sixteen years or so to pull it all together.

"How do we do *that?*" Jan asks for both of them. "Sell every-thing we own? Take three jobs?"

"I have about $35,000 in my 401(k)," Patrick offers. "And we have a few thousand in other savings. If we cash it out and buy lot-tery tickets . . ."

Jan punches his arm playfully, with exaggerated chagrin. They're having some fun with the startling news. A defense mechanism? That's all right. Better than an aneurysm. It *is* serious business, but it warrants neither panic nor depression.

"Moving in with the kids is looking better and better," muses Patrick. "Either that, or we both work till we're ninety-five."

Which settles both of them down fast and gets them focused on the task at hand.

"Can we really save what we need? Is it possible in our situation—with our bills?"

YOUR TOP FINANCIAL PRIORITY

Perhaps you're feeling a bit like Patrick and Jan today. You've calculated the nest egg you're likely to need for New Retirement, and it's one sizable egg. You've surveyed potential outside sources of laterlife income—Social Security, defined-benefit corporate pensions, and inheritances—and conservatively factored them into your planning. But the big nest egg you'll need upon Commencement Day still looms large. You, too, may be thinking, *Are you kidding me? Is it possible to get there?*

The purpose of our next few chapters is to assure you that your financial prospects for New Retirement can indeed be very promising. I don't want to mislead you, however. I'm not saying that building financial independence will be easy. As we concluded in chapter 3, none of us should rely solely on Social Security, pensions, or inheritances to supply all the income our New Retirement life style is going to require. *The level of financial freedom you achieve is completely up to you.*

Building what you need to pursue New Retirement dreams *will* take diligence on your part—sound strategy combined with discipline and a positive outlook. The fact is that if you're over thirty-five, saving and investing for New Retirement should be your top financial priority. If you're older and perhaps getting a later start, your situation will require greater effort. But whether you're thirty-five or sixty, it's better to start today than someday, better to apply sound strategy than haphazard hope.

HOW MUCH SHOULD YOU BE SAVING *NOW?*

One very reassuring truth in all this is that you will not need to save every dollar of your Big Sum—only a portion of the total. Although it's up to you to set funds aside, you're going to have several powerful allies to help your money accumulate much faster than the mere principal you save. We'll meet those allies in the next chapter. Today, it's vital that you acknowledge a key principle: All the positive market forces in the world can do you no good if you don't set aside the funds in the first place. Disciplined saving is where financial success begins.

> SAVING:
> the act of setting money aside for the future.
>
> INVESTING:
> putting that money to work to grow over time.
>
> You cannot INVEST successfully
> unless you first SAVE successfully.

❑ In your younger earning years you should start setting aside a portion of your gross annual income for New Retirement, both to get the compounding snowball rolling and to harness the tax advantages. The more you save in your early years, the less you'll need to scramble in your midlife years.

❑ If you are over thirty-five, saving for laterlife is your top financial priority.

❑ As you grow older, you'll want to become more focused and assertive by setting aside increasing percentages of your gross annual income.

❑ Do everything you can to meet the following long-term savings guidelines:

Figure 4.1

AMOUNT OF GROSS ANNUAL INCOME TO SAVE FOR LATERLIFE

Up to age 35	At least 5%
Age 35 to 45	At least 10%
Age 45 to 55	At least 15%
Age 55+	At least 20%

How do you measure up? If your present level of retirement savings falls short of those targets, I've prepared this chapter especially with you in mind. Like Patrick and Jan, you may think that increasing your savings commitment is impossible. But Patrick and Jan were wrong. Much to their delight, they were able to adjust their long-term savings to their target level *by locating money they didn't realize they had*. I have a very good feeling that you, too, can find several hundred dollars—possibly several thousand—that you didn't realize were available to you. Dollars you can pull out of limbo and direct toward your long-term savings program.

"FOUND MONEY"

Found money is a term used to describe available dollars a business or individual may not be aware of but is, in effect, in possession of. If your company has budgeted $250,000 for a new phone system but gets it for $200,000, the $50,000 is found money. It was considered gone, but now it's available for other purposes. If you submit a tax return claiming a refund of $700 and the IRS, benevolent institution that it is, sends you $1,200 because you forgot a deduction you were entitled to, the extra $500 is found money to you. (I wouldn't plan too heavily on the IRS doing such a thing. This is just an illustration.)

If you're like most people, there is indeed some found money sitting around in your life—money you may not be fully aware of, idle money that can be used to jump-start or accelerate your New Retirement savings program. Today we're going to help you discover those dollars. If you've been thinking that your monthly cash flow makes saving for the future difficult, if not impossible, you may be in for a pleasant surprise!

Ready to find some money and put it to work?

1. SEARCH HOME, OFFICE, CAR

That's right, we begin simply—searching room to room for loose change. Do not make the mistake of assuming that this won't make much difference, for small change can grow to big found money! Check wallets, dressers, cabinets, hutches, desk drawers, countertops, and under cushions, rounding up all the loose change you find. Perhaps, years ago, you tucked away a jar or piggy bank of pennies, nickels, and dimes—now's the time to dig it out. Search your vehicles for any loose change you may have tossed into ashtrays or coin trays or which may have slipped under the front seat. Likewise, check the nooks and crannies of your office work station for any coins you may have stashed there.

If you're like most people, this simple step will find you a minimum of $10 to $15. Some are pleasantly surprised to discover $50 or $60 sitting around. A one-time investment of $50, placed in a tax-deferred investment averaging a 10 percent return, will grow to $541.74 over twenty-five years. Find and invest $50 in loose change *once every year* for twenty-five years, and it will compound to more than $5,400. Small change, big potential.

2. EMPTY YOUR POCKETS

Now that you've rounded up your loose change and invested it, let's make the loose-change strategy a daily discipline. On almost any given day, you come home from work or from a round of errands with a small fistful of loose change in your pocket. Say that on a typical evening you return home with three quarters, a dime, two nickels, and three pennies: 98 cents. Some days you'll have more, some days less, so we'll consider 98 cents an average day.

Each evening, empty your pocket or wallet or purse of all the coins you've accumulated during the day. Place them in a jar and watch what happens. Ninety-eight cents per day adds up to $6.86 in one week. At the end of one month, your 98 cents per day will total $30 or so. Invested each month at 10 percent, this daily loose change will grow to almost $40,000 in twenty-five years.

If you want, you can stop at loose change. But, just for the fun of it, what would happen if you added just one of the dollar bills in your pocket, wallet, or purse each evening? In a week it becomes $13.86. In a month it's almost $60. In twenty-five years, invested at 10 percent, it will grow to more than $79,600!

It's a painless, effective habit. The only requirements: patience and loose change. I know couples who virtually funded their children's college education in this way. Over time, those little handfuls of pocket change can grow to thousands of dollars.

3. RETHINK YOUR HABITS

Just about everyone has at least one habit that can add up to lots of money. A $3 gourmet coffee each weekday morning adds up to $66 per month or $792 per year. Buying a daily $6 lunch instead of brown-bagging it totals $132 each month, $1,584 for the year.

Smoking just one pack of cigarettes per day wastes about $100 per month or $1,200 per year. And that's just for the cigarettes themselves. Keep in mind that smokers also pay nearly double what nonsmokers pay for life-insurance premiums and that smokers and those around them are likely to choke on some unwieldy medical bills in the future. Any way you light it, you're burning big bucks.

One extra $25 dinner out per month totals $300 per year. Adding two $5 desserts to that tab totals an additional $120 per year. An extra movie for two each month, with two medium popcorns and two medium soft drinks, can run $26 or more or $312 per year.

Are you spotting some possible found money here? What new money would you discover for saving and investing if you could

❑ brew your own coffee or endure the coffee at work—and make Starbucks a once-a-week treat (perhaps Friday mornings, as your reward for a productive week)?

❑ ease yourself out of the coffee habit altogether?

❑ pack a light, healthy lunch instead of lunching out each day?

❑ stop smoking?

❑ resist one extra dinner out every month?

❑ decline the expensive appetizers, alcoholic beverages, and desserts aggressively offered at nearly every restaurant?

❑ wait to rent most movies instead of going to the movie theater?

❑ wash your vehicles yourself instead of paying $3 to $10 for someone else to wash them?

❑ reduce the frequency of shopping trips, long drives, and long-distance phone calls (and rediscover the joy of writing and receiving letters)?

❑ cut back on nice-but-unnecessary groceries such as chips and dips, alcoholic and soft beverages, candy, designer drinking water, and prepared dinners?

To encourage you to rethink your habits, consider the long-range impact of just one of the above examples. Reducing the frequency of your morning Starbucks fix from one each weekday to one per week would save you about $12 per week, roughly $48 per month. Invested monthly at 10 percent, this one habit-shift will grow to about $603 per year. Over twenty-five years, it compounds to $63,688! Do the math on your other habits, and you'll be amazed at the amount of money you didn't realize you have.

4. SELL SOME STUFF

What little-used items clutter your home? Is there an extra vehicle (or two) that isn't really necessary but is draining cash for payments, registration, insurance, gas, oil, and repairs? What about rarely used motorcycles, bikes, RVs, boats, Jet Skis, skis, in-line skates, exercise equipment, tools, or books you'll never read again? Perhaps you've hung on to an old TV set, CD or tape player, or a CD or video collection.

Survey your place for at least three items you could sell for a hundred dollars or more, then place a classified ad and post fliers on the bulletin boards at work. You also may discover that you've accumulated enough stuff to stage a profitable garage sale. Do this once each year and steer the resulting found money to your long-term investments. Just one $300 lump sum each year, invested at 10 percent over twenty-five years, grows to $29,504.

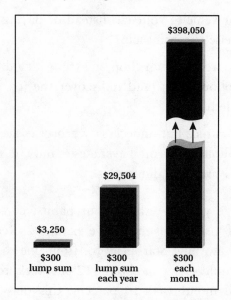

Figure 4.2
SMALL DOLLARS, BIG RESULTS
The result of savings invested at 10 percent over 25 years

5. TURN LIABILITIES INTO ASSETS

Next to procrastination, the biggest deterrent to financial freedom is consumer debt—the money you owe for all those just-had-to-have items purchased with credit cards.

Make no mistake, credit card companies absolutely *love* to loan you money on their Buy Now, Pay Forever plan. The more you borrow, the better—and they're so gracious about it that they'll even let you pay them back in tiny monthly installments. Aren't they nice? Not really. You've likely noticed that your friendly credit card issuers add a finance charge to your balance each month—annualized interest of 16, 18, even 20 percent of the outstanding balance. At 18 percent, a balance averaging $3,000 over the year means $540 in interest payments from your pocket to theirs. The higher the balance, the higher the interest. The higher the interest, the bigger your credit issuer's profits. The bigger your issuer's profits, the poorer your bank account and cash flow. No wonder these nice folk encourage high balances ("Charge that dream vacation now!") and small, easy monthly payments!

In chapter 9 I'll show you a sound strategy for getting rid of consumer debt—for good. I say "for good" intentionally because the result is just that: When you eliminate consumer debt you turn all those debt-servicing dollars into YOU-servicing dollars. Money that was paying for your past can now be invested for your future. Instead of paying interest, you can now earn interest. Found money!

6. STOP GIVING UNCLE SAM FREE LOANS

If you're among the millions who receive a tax refund of several hundred dollars every spring, you've allowed our beloved Uncle to overwithhold taxes from each paycheck. In other words, you're giving him more money than you're legally obligated to pay. It's like a loan, actually—a loan that Uncle will indeed pay back in good time, if you ask nicely. But the interest you earn on this loan is . . . zero percent. That's right. He pays absolutely nothing for the use of your money. (Try withholding tax money from *him* at zero interest.)

Question 1: Does this make sense?

Question 2: Is this good stewardship?

I realize we get a warm, fuzzy feeling when those refund checks arrive. But if you're like most refundees, you also have plans for those refunds—bills to pay, new toys to buy. Rarely does a tax refund find its way into long-term savings and investments. I encourage you to change that pattern by turning interest-free loans to Uncle Sam into found money for your investment program. It's simple to do.

Say you receive a paycheck every other week and your latest tax refund was $1,300. This means you allowed the feds to overwithhold $50 from each paycheck. Go to your tax consultant or your company's payroll person and have her help you calculate a new withholding allowance to keep that extra $50 from going to Uncle Sam each payday. She'll help you fill out a Form W-4, "Calculation of Withholding Allowance."

After you've adjusted your withholding allowances, you'll want to take immediate, proactive steps to redirect this found money toward long-term savings and investments. If you haven't yet maximized your contribution to your company's retirement savings plan, this is your top priority. Ask your payroll person for a form to steer this additional money into your 401(k) program. If you're already maxing out your company program, direct this extra money toward an IRA. (We'll discuss company programs and IRAs in greater detail in chapter 10.)

Adjusting withholding allowances is a simple, effective way to turn no-interest IRS loans into found money. It can provide more dollars each pay period to direct toward investments that work for *your* benefit instead of Uncle's. You won't have a huge tax refund next spring, but that's just the point: Your goal is to come close to break-even at tax time and put your money to wiser use in the meantime.

7. SAVE HUNDREDS ON INSURANCE

As a personal finance specialist, I'm a strong believer in the savvy use of insurance to provide for you and your loved ones in the event of a major loss. By investing a relatively small sum each year, we ensure that at least part of a designated, future financial catastrophe will be paid or reimbursed by the insurer, thus limiting our personal risk of a huge financial loss.

But, like many good things, insurance also has its drawbacks—among them all kinds of bells and whistles that may sound nice in the sales pitch but are usually unnecessary. Such bells and whistles, of course, cost you extra premium dollars. In many cases, those extra premiums add up to hundreds, even thousands, of dollars that could be put to much better use. For example . . .

❑ *Do you have whole life, variable life, or universal life insurance instead of level-premium term life insurance?* Except for a few rare instances, whole, variable, and universal life insurance are extremely poor uses of your life-insurance money. Insurance companies push them because they are high-commission, high-profit products; those commissions and profits come right out of your high premium. The "investment" features of such plans wilt from embarrassment when compared to investments you can easily make yourself. In the vast majority of cases, you'll receive far greater value for your dollar with a level-premium term life-insurance policy—much higher coverage, much lower premium. The difference in cost to you will be astounding.

❑ *Do you carry life insurance on your children?* The chief purpose of life insurance is to help replace family income that is lost when a breadwinner dies. It's virtually "income replacement" insurance. Does a child provide income essential to his or her family? Probably not. Tragic as losing a child is, such a loss is not a loss of essential income. Therefore, it makes little sense to carry life insurance on a child.

❑ *Do you carry credit life, mortgage life, or dread-disease insurance?* You've received the sales pitches: "Protect your loved ones: For just $4.95 per month, we'll pay off your credit card balance if you die." Or "Be sure your dear wife and children don't go homeless: For just $130 per month, we'll pay your mortgage in full if you die." Or "Important Alert! Your health insurance may not cover deadly Ingrown Toenail Syndrome.

For just $35 a month, we'll help you pay for expensive ITS."
Such specialty insurance is rarely a good value for the consumer, which is exactly why companies pitch it with gusto.

❑ *Do you fail to shop around for your life, auto, and homeowners insur-*
ance? Premiums for the same coverage can differ by hundreds
of dollars from policy to policy, company to company. It pays
to comparison-shop.

❑ *Do you carry low deductibles on auto or homeowners insurance?* The
lower the deductible, the higher your premium. Increase
deductibles to a minimum of $500; $1,000 will save you even
more as long as you have adequate savings to cover such contingencies.

❑ *Do you carry collision coverage on older cars?* Regardless of the
extent of damage, insurance companies won't pay more than
the book value of your vehicle, so consider whether collision
premiums are worth the payout you're likely to receive.

❑ *Do you fail to take full advantage of available discounts?* Carry
your homeowners, auto, and personal liability policies with
the same insurer and receive a multiple-policy discount.
Protect your home with deadbolt locks, a fire extinguisher,
and smoke detectors and receive an additional homeowners
policy discount. Ask about any auto insurance discounts that
may apply to you. Many insurers offer discounts to people
who are over fifty-five or have good driving records or whose
cars have air bags, antilock brakes, or antitheft devices.

❑ *Do you purchase insurance features you don't really need?* Car
insurers like to add riders covering towing and reimburse-
ments for emergency car rentals; generally you'll do better
with your AAA membership while avoiding the hassle of
insurance claims. Life insurers like to add an "accidental
death" rider with its promise that if you die as a result of an
accident, your beneficiary will receive double the death benefit. Don't gamble on your mode of death—calculate the death

benefit your dependents need, then purchase that amount—no less, no more.

Insurers also recommend a "waiver of premium" rider that will continue to pay your premiums if you become disabled. This can be a nice feature if you're the prime provider for your family and short on disability coverage and savings. But it's also a profit maker for insurance companies. I won't advise you to waive this rider, but it's something you might consider if your disability insurance and savings reserves are adequate.

❑ *Do you carry extended warranties on appliances?* Definitely a profit maker for the companies that issue them and a poor value for the consumer. Yes, we've all heard horror stories of appliances that go kaput six days after the manufacturer's warranty expires; kaputs do happen. But the odds really are in the insurer's favor, which warranty companies bank on. Your premiums are money in their pockets. The purpose of insurance is to protect you against catastrophic loss, not against minor expenses or inconveniences. Keep your savings reserves in good shape for the occasional kaputs and put extended-warranty premiums in your own pocket.

What would happen if you were to use the above list to evaluate and adjust your insurance coverage? It's typical to find anywhere from $300 to $3,000 in annual savings *without a meaningful decrease in the quality of your coverage.* Twelve hundred dollars of savings per year, invested faithfully, will grow to more than $118,000 over twenty-five years.

8. OFFER A SERVICE

Most likely you have a hobby or skill you can turn into a money-maker in your spare time, such as carpentry, baby-sitting, handyman work, typing, computer setup and tutoring, desktop publishing, writing, or photography. Are you a musician? Then offer singing lessons or teach a musical instrument. Do you like to make dried-flower arrangements or wall hangings? Are you adept at auto repair, small electrical jobs, plumbing? How about a family yard-maintenance business on the side? Sprinkler system start-up and shutoff? Snow shoveling or hanging Christmas lights?

You can make money with just about any hobby, skill, or service that comes to mind. To sell products consider flea markets, mall and trade shows, or home craft parties. To sell services, place ads on bulletin boards at work, distribute fliers in your neighborhood, and tell friends and neighbors you're available for a fair sum. Found money!

DON'T LOSE FOUND MONEY

If you're a somewhat normal person, your first inclination may be to respond to found money in the following calm and rational manner: "OHBOY,MONEY!LET'SGOCELEBRATEANDBUYTHISANDPUTA-DOWNPAYMENTONTHAT!AFTERALLWEOWEITTOOURSELVES!!!"

I don't want to spoil your fun. Really. But keep in mind that our purpose in locating found money is to provide you with funds you didn't realize you have to invest for your future. Indeed, the main reason we're on this search is that you may already have let too many dollars slip through your fingers in the first place.

So I'd like you to make yourself a promise. Promise yourself that you will put at least 70 to 80 percent of every chunk of found money to work for the long term. Rise above the normal temptation to spend it. Immediately write a check to steer any found money toward savings and investments. By doing so, you'll not only remove the temptation from your reach, but you'll also take one step closer to a financially independent retirement through the extraordinary power of compounding.

As the bumper sticker says, why be normal?

---

9. GET RID OF PMI

Not a hormonal condition, though almost as annoying, PMI is the vernacular for private mortgage insurance. If you're buying your house and you put down less than 20 percent of the purchase price, your lender may have saddled you with PMI, which protects him if you default on your loan. The premium for private mortgage insurance is added to your monthly mortgage payment and can run anywhere from $50 up to hundreds of dollars per month.

Once your home equity surpasses 20 percent of the original purchase price, you can drop private mortgage insurance. Until recently, lenders have made extra millions because they were not required to tell you when your equity was sufficient to cancel the coverage. You had to request cancellation, and you had to ask very nicely. In 1998 Congress passed legislation requiring lenders to automatically cancel PMI once a borrower's equity reaches 22 percent of the property's original value—a positive step, but effective only on loans originated on or after July 29, 1998. In 1999 Fannie Mae, the country's primary source of mortgage capital, announced that it will require lenders to automatically cancel PMI once a mortgage reaches midterm. This requirement is retroactive to existing mortgages, but mortgage lenders have until January 2001 to comply.

If you carry private mortgage insurance and believe your equity has surpassed 20 percent of the original loan, write your lender requesting that the coverage be dropped. He'll send you some paperwork, but your effort will be worth it. Reclaiming those dollars will enable you to invest another $50+ per month, or $600+ per year, toward your New Retirement.

10. CONSIDER REFINANCING

If interest rates have fallen since you secured your home mortgage loan, or if you have an adjustable rate mortgage that's moving skyward, you may be a good candidate to refinance your mortgage.

To refinance simply means to take out a new, lower-interest loan on your home and, in the process, pay off your old, higher-interest loan. Over the thirty-year life of the loan, the lower rate can save you tens of thousands of dollars in interest—money you can put to work for your family's future instead of the lender's. However, even though the interest rate is lower, the up-front costs of refinancing (such as "points" or origination fees, appraisals, and other fingers in the pie) can total several thousand dollars. Thus you want to be fairly sure you'll continue residing in the house long enough to earn back in lower monthly payments what you're paying out to refinance.

You'll find that refinance rates and costs vary widely. Call at least five mortgage lenders in your area to check their fees as well as their current rates on a thirty-year, fixed mortgage. Depending on the local economy and your situation, you may be able to refinance your mortgage and significantly reduce your monthly payments.

11. ACCELERATE YOUR MORTGAGE PRINCIPAL

This is a big-picture strategy that won't give you ready cash today, but it could give you *tens of thousands* of dollars over the next couple of decades. If you anticipate staying in your house a long time, even paying it off and owning it free and clear, consider accelerating your mortgage payoff to build equity (ownership) faster.

There are a couple of ways to do so. The simplest, though it has its drawbacks, is to take a fifteen-year or twenty-year fixed mortgage instead of the usual thirty-year. Interest rates on such loans are slightly lower; however, principal payments are naturally higher because there is less time to pay off the principal. Thus, a shorter-term mortgage won't do much to loosen up your monthly cash flow—but if owning your home free and clear is a priority for you, this course will help you get there faster. And in the long run, you will save many tens of thousands of dollars in interest payments.

A second approach requires a bit more effort on your part, but it's much more flexible. Let's assume you have a thirty-year, fixed-rate mortgage loan. Starting next month, write your check for an additional $25, $50, $100, or more. Specify on the statement that the additional amount goes to principal. (Most mortgage companies provide a space on their monthly statement or coupon for you to do so.)

You can do this every month or only on occasion—it's up to you. The result is a speedier reduction of the principal balance on which you owe interest. Depending on the size of your mortgage, how long you've had it, your interest rate, and the amount of additional principal you send each month, you can trim years off your payment schedule and save tens of thousands, possibly *hundreds of thousands,* in interest on the loan. Found money? It's not money in your pocket right now, but it's tons of money over time.

Perhaps the greatest potential benefit of accelerated mortgage payments is the possibility of owning your home free and clear in your later years. It also comes in handy if you decide to sell your home or take out a reverse mortgage (which we'll explore in chapter 13) to enhance your retirement cash flow.

12. BANK THOSE RAISES AND BONUSES

C. Northcote Parkinson, author of the famed "Parkinson's Law" ("Work expands to fill the time available"), also observed, "Expenses rise to meet income." He's right on both counts, but the second law explains human nature when it comes to personal finance. It seems that whenever we receive a raise, our monthly expenses rise to quickly consume it. If we're fortunate enough to earn a bonus, our needs or greeds devour the bonus as well. It can get downright discouraging.

In order to counter human nature's natural "laws," we have to take deliberate steps to be sure we respond more constructively when opportunities arise. Indeed, we *can* keep our expenses below our income, but it does take some predetermined discipline. We *can* preserve the bulk of any raises and bonuses for our long-term benefit.

Next time you receive a raise, pay yourself first. Begin steering 70 to 80 percent of the increase toward your investments. Use an automatic payroll deduction if your company offers one; otherwise, write that check to your savings and investment program as soon as your paycheck is deposited. Maintain 20 to 30 percent of the raise to increase your charitable giving, eliminate debt, and handle the rising cost of life's necessities.

If you receive a bonus, employ a similar strategy. Pay yourself first by sending 70 to 80 percent to your long-term savings and investments. Then take the remaining 20 or 30 percent, peel off a few tens to celebrate, then give, reduce a consumer debt, or increase your short-term savings.

13. OK, HOW ABOUT A BAKER'S DOZEN?

Hey, you're doing great, so why stop now? I realize I promised twelve places to find money for your future, but here's another for a "baker's dozen." Actually, it's a potpourri of ideas. (So I get carried away.) Can you find some additional savings in the following areas?

- ❑ *Shop for no-fee banking.* Many banks waive the monthly service charge on checking accounts if your employer deposits your paycheck directly. Also avoid banks that assess per-check service charges or ATM transaction fees. Banks want your patronage, so there are plenty of free alternatives out there.

- ❑ *Avoid ATM fees* by using only your bank's automated teller machine. If your own bank starts charging you, move to a bank that doesn't.

- ❑ *How many TVs, phone lines, and phone extensions does your family really need?* I realize I may be treading on sacred ground here, but I call 'em the way I see 'em, and a personal TV set, phone line, or phone extension for each child—even when limited to older children—is ludicrous. Not only are they a fiscal extravagance, they also encourage children to retreat into private shells instead of sharing time with the rest of the family. If you're among those on whom I have trodden, what might you rescue in both dollars and relationships by cutting back?

❑ *Sure, the cell phone is convenient. It's also expensive.* And dangerous, if you use it while driving—which may just mushroom to even bigger expenses. Necessity or luxury?

❑ *How many cable TV services do you really need and use?* How much would you save, and how little would you sacrifice, by cutting back to basic service?

❑ *How many telephone add-on services do you pay for each month?* Do you really need caller ID, voice messaging, call waiting, and whatever wonderful-sounding new service the phone company will roll out next month?

❑ *Consider a low-cost, stay-at-home vacation.* If you've been draining your savings account on vacations or, worse, Master-Carding them, try rejuvenating "on the cheap" this year. Take time off from work, don't tell anyone where you're going, and laze around to your heart's content. Sleep in. (Turn your phones off.) Putter in the garden. Read a novel. (Don't call the office.) Go see a good movie. Enjoy a couple of meals out. Take a hike. (Don't call friends who work at your office.) Take a nap. Rent a black-and-white comedy classic. Visit a zoo or museum. (Don't drive past the office.) Fly a kite. Relax with non-office friends. Play miniature golf. You may discover, as many good folk do, that a "hang around" vacation is even more relaxing and rejuvenating than traveling somewhere. And definitely less expensive!

❑ *When buying groceries, prepare a list ahead of time . . . and stick to your plan.* List items in the order of your usual pattern through the store. Fair warning: Your grocery chain has spent millions figuring out how to lure you beyond your shopping list. And it's working: The average family of four spends $70 on unplanned, "impulse" groceries every week. Grocers place impulse items at eye level (yours and your children's), on end-caps (those piles of chips and soft drinks at the end of an aisle), and at checkout lanes. Stand firm.

❑ *Clip and use grocery coupons . . . but beware the common mistake of buying something only because you have a coupon for it.* That's just another form of impulse buying. Limit coupon use to items you would purchase anyway.

❑ *Don't grocery shop when hungry.* You spend 17 percent more when you shop on an empty stomach.

❑ *When grocery shopping, leave husbands and children at home if at all possible.* I don't have to cite studies here, do I? It's an unusual husband who does not add at least two impulse items to a grocery cart. (I plead guilty; I thought we really needed those M&Ms and cinnamon rolls.) It's an unusual child who does not loudly proclaim, at least once every five minutes and for extended periods in the checkout lane, that you are an unfit mother if you do not buy him whatever he's pointing to at the moment. Too many moms acquiesce out of embarrassment or weariness.

❑ *How many vehicles do you really need?* Stroll down a typical residential street and it seems most families have at least one vehicle for every driver in the house—plus the obligatory pickup truck or SUV. Not only are three-car garages full to overflowing, but more cars and trucks spill out onto driveways and cul-de-sacs. If this describes your garage and driveway, how many hundreds of dollars would you save each year if you sold just one of those vehicles? OK, what if you sold two? It might mean sharing some rides, but a little planning, communication, sharing, and conversation among family members won't hurt a bit. Could save you hundreds or more per year.

❑ *When buying a car, buy "almost new."* Most of a vehicle's depreciation takes place in its first two to three years, yet many cars and trucks are still in great shape after this period of time. So it makes financial sense to shop for a well-maintained, low-mileage vehicle that's just two or three years old.

(For obvious reasons you may want to avoid used police cars, taxicabs, and anything driven by pizza delivery guys.) Once you find something with the look and ride you like, have an independent mechanic give it a thorough physical. Then dicker! Depreciation will enable you to purchase an almost-new car for thousands less than new. Bonus: "Preowned" vehicles also cost less when it comes to annual registration and insurance.

MORE FOUND MONEY ALONG THE WAY

I hope this chapter has opened your mind to the probability that you have more money than you think you do—and how even small sums of found money, wisely invested, can compound into significant amounts to help make your retirement a financially independent one.

I hope, too, that I've stimulated you to rethink other aspects of your financial life from the perspective of finding extra dollars to help you eliminate debt and build long-term savings. You'll find it has a positive snowball effect: The more you locate and invest found money, the more additional areas of savings you will uncover.

Some of those discoveries await you in the pages that follow. As we proceed through *Never Retire,* keep your highlighter ready for more sources of money you didn't realize you have, whether it's from clearing debt, buying smarter, or saving and investing more wisely. Your found money could total thousands of dollars before we're through. Before *you're* through, it could total hundreds of thousands.

ACTION POINTS

Throughout *Never Retire* we've provided Action Points pages to help you personalize and apply what you're reading. Use these pages to record key steps you feel led to take in preparation for New Retirement.

HABITS I WANT TO CHANGE

-
-
-
-

NEW ATTITUDES I WANT TO LIVE BY

-
-
-
-

ACTION STEPS I NEED TO TAKE

1.
2.
3.
4.
5.

CAN I REALLY BE FINANCIALLY INDEPENDENT?

Reaching your goal may be more doable than you think.

Y ou are on your own, but you are not alone.

When it comes to preparing for New Retirement, this simple, seemingly contradictory statement sums up where most of us stand. We are indeed "on our own" because *it is up to us* to take the necessary steps to build financial freedom. No one else will do it for us. On the other hand, "we are not alone" because, once we begin taking those steps, there are some powerful allies available to help us turn our commitment into reality.

On our own, but not alone. I enjoy football, so please indulge me in a football fantasy to illustrate what I mean. We're running backs, you and I. (Don't fall out of your chair laughing.) It's our responsibility to embrace the game plan and run smartly to advance the ball to the goal line. Fortunately, we are not the only ones out there. We're surrounded by some powerful teammates, hard-hitting blockers who can help spring us loose for significant gains and game-winning touchdowns. Without our teammates, we're just your average running backs. With them, we can realistically think *end zone.*

On our own, but not alone.

On the field of personal finance, you have several "teammates" who can and will help you make the most of your effort to build financial independence. Working together, they can take a fistful of your dollars and, over time, help them grow and multiply. They can help turn what appears to be an inadequate puddle of savings into a large, full reservoir to fund your New Retirement.

So as you contemplate the question "Can I really be financially independent?" I think it will encourage you to meet seven of your teammates—and see how they can help make that faraway financial goal a reality. Don't let their names scare you or tempt you to skip-read. They're your friends. You *want* to know who they are and how they work. Here they are:

> Compound interest
> Tax deductibility
> Tax deferral
> Equity investments
> Simplicity
> Diversification
> Asset allocation

Once you've read their game stats, you won't want to invest another penny without them.

THE INCREDIBLE POWER OF COMPOUNDING

The "time value of money" is a dull-sounding accounting concept that can actually get exciting—especially when it's *your* money we're talking about. It simply means that a modest sum, invested at a given rate of return over a period of time, can grow into a surprisingly sizable amount.

The key is *compound interest*—the most powerful teammate we have in building the nest egg we will need. Say you make a one-time contribution of $2,000 to a tax-advantaged investment averaging 10 percent annual growth. After one year you'll have approximately $2,200. During the second year, you'll earn interest not only on your original $2,000, but also on the $200 you earned in year one. In other words, you're earning *interest on principal* and *interest on interest*. In this example, your $2,000 will compound to $2,420 by the end of year two.

In the big scheme of things, those dollars may seem insignificant. But if you leave the money alone and it continues averaging 10 percent, your original investment of $2,000 (with no additional principal added) will compound to more than $21,600 over twenty-five years. A tenfold increase—small change, big results!

Now take the power of compounding a step further. Consider what happens if you contribute $2,000 *each year* for the same period of time. Figure 5.1 shows how, at 10 percent average annual return, $2,000 per year grows to more than $216,300 over twenty-five years. If you can invest $4,000 annually, you'll end up with $432,700. Set aside $6,000 per year, and in twenty-five years you will have almost $650,000.

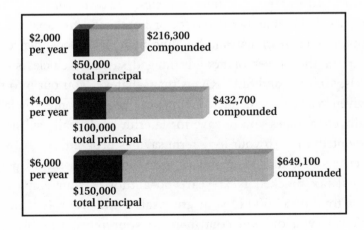

Figure 5.1

THE INCREDIBLE POWER OF COMPOUNDING

Annual investments averaging 10 percent over 25 years

To make compounding especially mouth-watering, Figure 5.1 also shows the relationship between your principal contribution and your total compounded results. Over twenty-five years, at $2,000 per year, you contribute a total of $50,000 to retirement savings. Yet your total compounded result is more than $216,000; the power of compounding gives you $166,000 in free money. At $4,000 per year, you set aside a total of $100,000; compounding gives you $332,700 free. At $6,000 per year, your total principal is $150,000; compounding provides you with a free $500,000. No wonder Albert Einstein, a fair student of numbers himself, dubbed compound interest the most powerful natural force in the world!

In Part Two we'll discuss where to find the best tax-advantaged savings vehicles and investments. For now, I want you to take hope in how relatively small dollars can compound into big results. You just may come to believe that the time value of money isn't so dull anymore!

THE POWER OF TAX DEDUCTIBILITY

In the above examples of the power of compounding, we were using tax-advantaged savings vehicles. *Tax-advantaged* simply means tax-deductible, tax-deferred, or both—and fortunately, both are among your teammates in building financial independence.

Part of the power of tax-advantaged savings vehicles such as 401(k)s, 403(b)s, and SEP-IRAs is that whatever you put into them in a given year can be deducted from your gross income. Uncle Sam actually encourages you to save for laterlife by literally subsidizing your contribution to your long-term savings program.

Let's assume that your income level puts you in the 15 percent marginal tax bracket. Next year you authorize your employer to direct a total of $3,000 of your gross salary into your 401(k).

Now if you did *not* contribute to your retirement plan, you would pay an income tax of $450 on that $3,000 (15 percent of $3,000 = $450). Fortunately, according to current law, your contribution to a 401(k), 403(b), or SEP-IRA program is *tax deductible*—you do not pay income tax on the amount. (Contributions to regular IRAs may or may not be deductible; see chapter 10 for guidance.) With tax deductibility running interference for you, steering $3,000 of your gross salary to your 401(k) saves you $450 in income taxes. In effect, you'll contribute just $2,550; Uncle Sam will dip into his own coat pocket and toss $450 into the kitty for you.

What if your income puts you in the 28 percent marginal bracket and you decide to set aside $6,000? Without the 401(k) contribution, you would owe income tax of $1,680 on the $6,000. With the contribution, you effectively contribute $4,320 while Uncle pitches in $1,680.

Hey, the IRS isn't exactly known for being helpful, so we ought to take full advantage when it does offer incentives as powerful as tax deductibility. Consider it our federal government's way of admitting that we individuals must indeed take responsibility to save for our future. It's so vital that Uncle Sam offers to help by making our retirement-savings contributions tax-deductible. Found money!

THE POWER OF TAX DEFERRAL

Government incentive to save for retirement does not stop at tax deductibility. Even more powerful is *tax deferral*—which legally postpones income tax on investment earnings until we begin drawing income from those investments. 401(k)s, 403(b)s, IRAs, Roth IRAs, SEP-IRAs, and annuities all allow us to defer taxes on investment earnings.

After witnessing the incredible effect of compounding shown above, you can better appreciate what tax deferral means to your savings and investment program. Because compounding earns interest on principal *and interest on interest,* interest sheltered from taxation means more money working for you over time—earning even more interest! Look at the comparison in Figure 5.2:

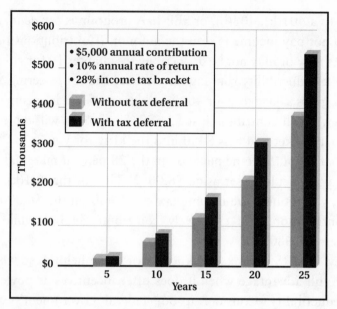

Figure 5.2
THE POWER OF TAX DEFERRAL
The effect of tax-deferral vs. non-tax-deferral on savings averaging 10 percent annual return over 25 years

The difference between tax-deferred and non-tax-deferred savings is dramatic and demonstrates why it's wise to maximize contributions to every tax-deferred savings vehicle available to us before adding to non-tax-deferred accounts. As we will see in Part Two, you may be eligible for *multiple* tax-advantaged savings plans, which will increase your ability to save as aggressively as necessary to meet your long-term goal.

THE POWER OF EQUITY INVESTING

We'll address investing in greater detail as we study the Seven Pillars of Financially Independent Retirement, but a quick overview here will show how, combined with the efforts of compounding, tax deductibility, and tax deferral, *equity investing* helps our money grow the way we need it to.

Whittle investing down to its bare bones and you find two basic types of investments: *ownership* (or *equity*) investments and *loanership* (or *debt*) investments. Ownership means you actually use your dollars to buy a portion of a company's stock—you are literally a part owner. For example, if you participate in a 401(k) plan that invests in a growth or growth-and-income mutual fund, chances are you own shares of Microsoft. You're a co-owner with Bill Gates! He owns a few more shares than you do, so he's still the boss, but you indeed have *equity* in Microsoft. You participate in and benefit from the growth in share value of the company's stock. If you had invested in Microsoft back when young, precocious Bill started the company in his college dorm room, you'd now own a *ton* of equity in Microsoft but none of your friends would be speaking to you.

The downside of ownership investments is that you also participate in any *declines* in corporate share value. Therefore, equity investments offer higher potential reward but also higher potential risk. As we all know, stock market indices such as the Dow Jones Industrial Average, NASDAQ, and Standard & Poor's 500 go up and down from week to week, reflecting investor sentiment about the potential of specific companies and the economy in general. But though the market has both *bull* (upward) and *bear* (downward) trends, its overall long-term direction has been bullish, averaging better than 10 percent annual return since 1926 and more than 12 percent since 1946. When you consider that these averages include the Great Depression and several "crashes" since, their long-term performance isn't too shabby! Although downward swings can occur at any time and may, in fact, be occurring as you read this, the long-range trend of the equities market can give us some degree of assurance of long-term growth of our money.

Loanership or *debt* investments are far more conservative—less risk, less reward. When you purchase a bond, for example, you virtually loan a chunk of money to the issuer for a specified period of time at a specified rate of return. The bond you receive is an IOU through which the borrower pledges to pay you the specified interest on a periodic basis then return the principal amount at the end of the term. Many loanership investments can also be called *income investments* because older investors purchase them in order to provide a somewhat reliable, though less than spectacular, stream of monthly or quarterly income.

On the surface, bond-based investments appear safer than equity investments. However, keep in mind that their returns are fixed at a specified rate much lower than the potential return of equity investments over time. In many cases, the payback on debt instruments may barely keep pace with inflation. This is why, in our early-adult and early-midlife years, it makes little sense to invest in debt investments. We have sufficient time on our side to ride out the stock market's inevitable ups and downs and earn a much better average return on our savings. Approximately ten to fifteen years from Commencement, depending on your situation, you may want to begin blending some bond-based investments into your portfolio to help mitigate potential stock market risk. Until then, equity investments are the way to go.

THE POWER OF SIMPLICITY

Don't get nervous if talk of the stock market tends to frighten you. We're going to keep equity investing simple by using mutual funds, not individual stocks, and by keeping most of our money within those tax-advantaged savings vehicles we've been talking about. One of the many advantages of mutual funds is that they provide professional management—seasoned stock selectors who make the daily buy-sell decisions for stocks owned by each fund. Basically, you select the fund that's right for you, then sit back and enjoy the ride. In chapter 11, "Put Your Savings to Work," we'll further explore what mutual funds are, how to invest in them, and types of funds for you to consider.

THE POWER OF DIVERSIFICATION

Remember your wise granddad telling you, "Don't put all your eggs in one basket"? He may not have realized it at the time, but he was recommending *diversification,* the act of spreading your resources among different companies and types of companies so that, if a few should encounter bad fortune, the others can sustain your principal and (hopefully) your growth.

It's another of those timeless truths that has stayed constant from biblical to modern times. Three thousand years ago, the wisest and wealthiest man in the world advised, "Divide your portion to seven, or even to eight, for you do not know what misfortune may occur on the earth" (Ecclesiastes 11:2, NASB).

Now if King Solomon were alive today, he would be very old. But he would also advise exactly the same thing as he did back then, for financial wisdom still calls for diversifying one's assets among several different investments or investment types. Amazing, when you think about it, that the Holy Bible is as relevant today as it was thousands of years ago. Someone really smart, with lots of foresight, must have supervised its authorship.

Heeding Solomon's counsel, we're going to achieve two levels of diversification as we invest our savings in mutual funds. First, a single mutual fund is already a diversified investment because it spreads its assets among at least twenty (usually more) different companies' stocks. Then we'll go one better and spread our assets among several different mutual funds to diversify the *types* of companies we own. There are never any guarantees in the investment business, but diversification goes a long way in spreading and compensating for downside risk.

THE POWER OF ASSET ALLOCATION

The strength and importance of our seventh teammate, *asset allocation,* was spotlighted in a watershed study by financial experts Gary P. Brinson, Brian D. Singer, and Gilbert Beebower in the early 1990s. After reviewing the long-term performance of dozens of stock portfolios and case studies, they concluded that, contrary to common thought, most profits from investments *do not* result from picking the right stock or from moving in and out of the market at the right time during up-and-down movements.

Instead, *most gains from the market result from selecting the right combination of investments.* Specifically, 92 percent of gains came from asset allocation (how you allocate your assets among various types of investments), while only 8 percent of gains resulted from market timing or the performance of a particular stock, bond, or mutual fund.

Again, this is heartening news for midlifers preparing for New Retirement. Not only do you gain additional safety through asset allocation, you also gain additional earning power.

Most mutual funds provide some degree of self-contained asset allocation by spreading assets among different types of industries; you can further enhance your asset allocation by investing among different mutual funds with differing objectives. If Brinson, Singer, and Beebower are right, proper asset allocation will have a dramatic effect on the long-range performance of your New Retirement savings.

PUT THEM ALL TOGETHER AND . . .

You are on your own, but you are not alone. With seven strong teammates running alongside you, reaching the end zone doesn't seem quite as daunting, does it? With the powers of compounding, tax deductibility, tax deferral, equity investing, simplicity, diversification, and asset allocation working together, the money you're able to set aside can achieve dramatic growth between now and Commencement Day.

As we wrap up this chapter, I invite you to check out the following tables, Figures 5.3 and 5.4. I know, I know, rows and rows of numbers—an accountant's dream and everyone else's nightmare. But these numbers are friendly and easy to use. They dramatically illustrate the time value of money—the incredible power of compounding over time. The tables are going to help you envision the possibilities of building the level of financial independence you desire for New Retirement. I think they will encourage you . . . or at least spur you to action.

You'll have several variables to work with. Figure 5.3 assumes your invested savings can average a 10 percent annual return over time, tax-deferred. Some years you'll earn more, and some years you'll earn less, but history tells us that over the long haul, 10 percent average compounded growth is a healthy, realistic target.

Figure 5.4 shows the big difference just two percentage points can make—a 12 percent average annual return as opposed to 10 percent. A recent Kiplinger report forecasts an average annual return of 12 percent for the Standard & Poor's 500 (an index of the top five hundred stocks in America) over the next several decades. It's possible that as the baby boomer generation continues to pour new capital into the markets, the average annual return on investment will go up—12 percent . . . 15 percent . . . who knows? So just for fun, play with the second table as well.

Here's how to apply these tables to your personal situation. Say you currently have $50,000 in tax-deferred retirement accounts, and New Retirement is at least twenty years away. You want to build a nest egg totaling $750,000 over the next twenty years. You think 10 percent is a nice average annual return to shoot for, so you look to Figure 5.3, 10% ANNUALIZED COMPOUNDED GROWTH.

❑ Under Lump Sum, find $50,000. Follow the line across the page to see what this sum will compound to over twenty years. The compounded total is $336,375—$413,625 short of your goal. Thus, your savings efforts from today forward will need to compound to approximately $413,625 to bring you to your goal in twenty years. (You can also use this section to estimate the long-term effect of any lump sums you may add to your savings in the future.)

❑ Go to the Monthly section, look down the 20 Years column, and find the first number to surpass $413,625 in twenty years. Trace that line to the left and, under Monthly, you'll see that a monthly contribution of $600 over the next twenty years will compound to $455,621. Add this total to your Lump Sum total, and you will have approximately $791,996 on Commencement Day. You've reached your goal!

❑ Use the Annual section if you foresee making yearly deposits to a tax-deferred retirement plan. Keep in mind that even if you have a 401(k)-type plan at work, you may also be able to contribute to a regular IRA or Roth IRA—or to a SEP-IRA if you have self-employment income.

❑ Now enter your own numbers, total the possibilities, and play with the variables. Do the same with Figure 5.4 to see what a 12 percent annual return will look like over ten, fifteen, twenty, twenty-five, and thirty years.

If your personalized numbers don't total what you think you'll need, see if you can increase your projected monthly or annual deposits. (The found money you rustled up in chapter 4 should help.) Could you take on some extra work and toss a nice new lump sum into the pot? What about postponing Commencement a few years to give your money more time to grow and compound? (Remember, "retirement age" is whenever *you* want it to be; no one says you must leave work at age sixty-five.)

On the other hand, as you play with the variables, you just may find your heart all aflutter—you may project having *more* than the Big Sum you've calculated or reaching your target sooner than anticipated. If so, rejoice! (This one's a good problem to have.) You could move your Commencement up a few years—enter New Retirement early, get busy pursuing your list of dreams. Or you could pull back a bit on your long-term savings efforts and devote more current money to debt elimination, travel, schooling, volunteer work, extra giving. Or you may wish to just maintain the status quo, building some additional financial cushion in case you live to be 120.

By adjusting the lump sums, monthly and annual deposits, length of time for compounding, and rates of return, you'll see that the Big Sum you once could hardly imagine may be a realistic goal after all. With determination and diligence on your part, combined with the help of your seven powerful teammates, financial independence *can* be part of your future!

Figure 5.3
10% ANNUALIZED COMPOUNDED GROWTH
(TAX-DEFERRED)

LUMP SUM	10 years	15 years	20 years	25 years	30 years
$2,500	6,484	10,443	16,818	27,087	43,624
$5,000	12,969	20,886	33,638	54,174	87,247
$10,000	16,105	25,937	67,275	108,347	174,494
$20,000	51,875	83,545	134,550	216,694	348,988
$30,000	77,812	125,317	201,825	325,041	523,482
$40,000	103,750	167,090	269,100	433,388	697,976
$50,000	129,687	208,862	336,375	541,735	872,470
$60,000	155,625	250,635	403,650	650,082	1,046,964
$70,000	181,562	292,407	470,925	758,429	1,221,458
$80,000	207,499	334,180	538,200	866,776	1,395,952
$90,000	233,437	375,952	605,475	975,124	1,570,446
$100,000	259,374	417,725	672,750	1,083,471	1,744,940
MONTHLY	10 years	15 years	20 years	25 years	30 years
$200	40,969	82,894	151,874	265,367	452,098
$300	61,453	124,341	227,810	398,050	678,146
$400	81,938	165,788	303,747	530,733	904,195
$500	102,422	207,235	379,684	663,416	1,130,244
$600	122,907	248,682	455,621	796,100	1,356,293
$700	143,391	290,129	531,558	928,783	1,582,342
$800	163,876	331,576	607,495	1,061,467	1,808,390
$900	184,360	373,023	683,432	1,194,150	2,034,439
$1,000	204,845	414,470	759,369	1,326,833	2,260,488
ANNUAL	10 years	15 years	20 years	25 years	30 years
$1,000	17,531	34,950	63,003	108,182	180,943
$2,000	35,062	69,899	126,005	216,364	361,887
$4,000	70,125	139,799	252,010	432,727	723,774
$5,000	87,656	174,749	315,013	540,909	904,717
$7,500	131,484	262,123	472,519	811,363	1,357,076
$10,000	175,312	349,497	630,025	1,081,818	1,809,434
$15,000	262,968	524,246	945,037	1,622,726	2,714,151
$20,000	350,623	698,995	1,260,050	2,163,635	3,618,869

Figure 5.4
12% ANNUALIZED COMPOUNDED GROWTH
(TAX-DEFERRED)

LUMP SUM	10 years	15 years	20 years	25 years	30 years
$2,500	7,765	13,684	24,116	42,500	74,900
$5,000	15,529	27,368	48,231	85,000	149,800
$10,000	31,058	54,736	96,463	170,001	299,599
$20,000	62,117	109,471	192,926	340,001	599,198
$30,000	93,175	164,207	289,389	510,002	898,798
$40,000	124,234	218,943	385,852	680,003	1,198,397
$50,000	155,292	273,678	482,315	850,003	1,497,996
$60,000	186,351	328,414	578,778	1,020,004	1,797,595
$70,000	217,409	383,150	675,241	1,190,005	2,097,195
$80,000	248,468	437,885	771,703	1,360,005	2,396,393
$90,000	279,526	492,621	868,166	1,530,006	2,696,393
$100,000	310,585	547,357	964,629	1,700,006	2,995,992
MONTHLY	10 years	15 years	20 years	25 years	30 years
$200	46,008	99,916	197,851	375,769	698,993
$300	69,012	149,874	296,777	563,654	1,048,489
$400	92,015	199,832	395,702	751,539	1,397,986
$500	115,019	249,790	494,628	939,423	1,747,482
$600	138,023	299,748	593,553	1,127,308	2,096,978
$700	161,027	349,706	692,479	1,315,193	2,446,475
$800	184,031	399,664	791,404	1,503,077	2,795,971
$900	207,035	449,622	890,330	1,690,962	3,145,468
$1,000	230,039	499,580	989,255	1,878,847	3,494,964
ANNUAL	10 years	15 years	20 years	25 years	30 years
$1,000	19,655	41,753	90,345	166,334	300,253
$2,000	42,415	88,980	171,044	315,668	570,545
$4,000	81,724	172,487	332,441	614,336	1,201,010
$5,000	110,696	230,661	442,079	814,670	1,471,303
$7,500	159,833	335,044	643,826	1,188,005	2,147,034
$10,000	196,546	417,533	806,987	1,493,339	2,702,926
$15,000	294,819	626,299	1,210,481	2,240,009	4,054,389
$20,000	393,092	835,066	1,613,975	2,986,679	5,405,852

SIX

MORE GOOD QUESTIONS

Real life is what happens when you've made other plans.

At last, a sparkle of hope in Jan's eyes.

She and Patrick have pored over the compounding tables and seen the possibilities over the next fifteen, twenty years. They've scoured their personal finances and located found money—both monthly and lump sums—to redirect to their New Retirement savings plans. This has enabled Patrick to increase his 401(k) contributions from 5 percent of his gross salary to 12 percent. He'll up that again, to 15 percent, when he receives his next salary increase in five months. They'll also be starting a plan for Jan at her place of employment and looking into personal IRAs.

Their Big Sum, which at first glance seemed so huge and impossible to attain, now appears reachable. It'll take discipline, determination, and some hard choices along the way. But the possibility of reaching "retirement age" (whatever age that may be for them) in a state of financial independence has put the sparkle in Jan's eyes.

Patrick's eyes have always had a mischievous twinkle, and today is no exception. But he looks like he has just a few more questions to ask. "So there's a light at the end of the tunnel," he ventures, "and hopefully it's not a train. But what if one of us loses our job? Or we have a big emergency . . . ?"

More good questions. We have a finite amount of money, and

real life tosses us an infinite variety of dilemmas that demand money. As a result, even the best-laid plans can become sidetracked. Today we're going to consider six commonly asked "good questions" dealing with financial dilemmas you may encounter as you set aside funds for your laterlife:

- "How do I handle financial emergencies?"
- "What will inflation do to my savings?"
- "Shouldn't I wait till my debts are all paid?"
- "What if I'm getting a late start?"
- "Shouldn't I wait till my kids are through college?"
- "What if I'll have dependent parents?"

"WHAT ABOUT THE MURPHS?"

The Murphs? We've encountered them before, and we will again.

The best way I can describe a Murph is with another football analogy. (When you write *your* book, you can use ice dancing, dogsledding, Yahtzee, whatever you wish. I won't mind. Just stay with me for this.) It's one of those hazy-crazy dreams . . . or *is* it a dream . . . the kind where reality blends with absurdity but it all seems so real. You and some friends are playing sandlot football and having a great time . . . your quarterback buddy flips the ball your way and you dash toward the goal line, the end zone in clear view. The only opponent between you and the goal line is little Ralphie Simmons, who plays flute in the school band and will fall over if you sneeze on him. You've got it made.

Then, as you draw closer, little Ralphie's demeanor begins to change . . . and in a split second the meek flutist morphs into . . . none other than Blitzkrieg Murphy, a.k.a. "the Murph." You know, the snarly linebacker released by the 1970s Oakland Raiders for playing too mean—and the Raiders *invented* mean.

You and your friends were just enjoying a friendly game of

touch, but Murphy doesn't believe in touch. He's decked in bull-like pads and pockmarked helmet. His bloodied, tattered jersey reads *Da Raidahs*. Blitzkrieg Murphy's as big as Stone Mountain and lurks smack-dab between you and where you want to go, his massive arms spread in sadistic welcome. And he's drooling. To cross the goal line, you've got to get past the Murph, preferably with your arms, legs, and head attached.

Good thing it's only a dream . . .

But personal finance can feel like that dream sometimes. Like you're running toward a goal, may even have it in sight, when all of a sudden a Murph looms before you, yearning to do you damage. You already know his credo too well: *"If anything can go wrong, it will."* And he likes to hang around just to make sure it does.

PREPARING FOR THE MURPHS

A Murph is any kind of personal financial setback we hadn't anticipated—a surprise layoff from work, a medical emergency, a big car repair, you name it. Instead of found money, the Murphs mean lost money—expenses we hadn't planned for. We've all encountered them, and we will again. As someone has wisely summed up, "Real life is what happens when you've made other plans."

The easiest, most obvious way to prepare for Murphs is to make sure our insurance coverages—life, health, disability, homeowners, auto, liability—are adequate and up-to-date. Good insurance policies can bear the brunt of many potentially devastating financial setbacks, though we're still on the hook for deductibles and copayments. We'll address this important area of financial planning in Part Two. But there are also many potential setbacks insurance does not cover.

Undoubtedly you've read or heard that most financial planners advise a liquid emergency reserve of three to six months' living expenses. When contingencies strike (and they will) you don't want to have to incur debt to pay for them. You *especially* don't want to pull money from your New Retirement savings program. Murphs are precisely why building a contingency reserve is good advice. Kept separate from your long-term savings, a contingency fund should be readily accessible in time of genuine need, yet not as accessible as, say, your bank ATM so you won't be tempted to pilfer it on whim. A money market fund is a perfect place for your contingency reserve.

WHERE TO BUILD A CONTINGENCY FUND

A *money market fund* is an ideal place to build a contingency reserve of three to six months' living expenses. It's a type of mutual fund that invests in a variety of conservative, short-term vehicles such as certificates of deposit, commercial paper, and U. S. government securities. The better ones will bring you higher returns than a bank savings account while maintaining your need for liquidity and preservation of principal. Unlike regular mutual funds, where your principal fluctuates according to market demand, a money market fund maintains the value of your original investment and pays monthly dividends on the earnings of its portfolio. It is *not* guaranteed or insured, but its investments are typically so conservative and short-term that financial experts deem most money market funds just as safe, and possibly safer, than insured bank accounts. If you're in a high tax bracket, you can choose a tax-free fund.

The money market fund you use will come with free check-writing privileges, usually for a minimum amount ranging from $100 to $500, and the option of making biweekly or monthly automatic deposits from your local checking account. It will require a minimum initial deposit of $500 to $1,000 or more (sometimes waived if you sign for the automatic deposit) and minimum subsequent deposits of $50 or more. You won't want to use a money market fund for everyday check writing; maintain your local checking account for that. But your money market fund will serve you well as a separate, convenient vehicle for building a contingency reserve.

Your contingency reserve is where you'll turn when the Murphs enter your financial life—so you can pay cash and avoid taking on more debt or raiding your New Retirement savings. Among the money market funds I like are:

- Prime Reserve Portfolio (The Vanguard Group) 800-662-7447

- Fidelity Cash Reserves (Fidelity Investments) 800-544-6666

- Prime Money Market Fund (American Century Investments) 800-345-2021

BUILDING A CONTINGENCY RESERVE

The natural question that arises is "Should I fund a contingency reserve *in full* before I start saving for the long term?" Experts disagree on this one. I've found that if you postpone long-term saving and investment until you build six months' expenses in liquid savings, chances are you'll delay too long in starting your long-term program. Building a three- to six-month reserve takes time, and as Murphs pop up along the way you end up taking one step forward, one step back. Meanwhile, as you're trying to build your contingency reserve, you're losing out on the powerful tax advantages and compounding power available through retirement savings programs.

So unless you're dripping with cash and can fully fund both a contingency reserve and long-term savings program at the same time, a compromise can help you address both needs simultaneously:

❏ If you haven't already done so, your first savings priority is to set aside several hundred dollars in a contingency reserve so you won't have to resort to debt when Murphs happen. Try to build $1,000 in a money market fund within the next six months, and do not withdraw any of this money for anything short of a real emergency.

❏ At the end of the last chapter, you saw the powerful effect of tax-deferred compounding—and you don't want to forego that effect for very long. So as soon as you've built $1,000 in your contingency reserve, begin setting aside at least 2 or 3 percent of your gross income in tax-advantaged retirement savings programs *as you continue to build your contingency fund*. Continue this pattern until you've built a contingency reserve equal to two months' living expenses.

❏ When your contingency reserve equals two months' expenses, begin increasing your contributions to your long-term savings by two or three percentage points each year. (Most 401(k) plans allow you to contribute up to 15 percent of your gross salary.) Meanwhile, continue adding to your contingency reserve to bring it up to the equivalent of three to six months' living expenses.

With this approach you'll grow several thousand in an accessible money market fund for those occasions when Blitzkrieg Murphy pops up to greet you. At the same time you can enjoy the tax-advantaged power of compounding with your retirement savings plans. Once your money market contingency reserve is equivalent to three to six months' expenses, you can leave it alone and turn to maxing out your contributions to retirement savings. And whenever a drooling Murph puts a ding in your contingency fund, replenish that amount as soon as possible to keep your liquid reserve at a comfortable level.

"WHAT ABOUT THE EFFECT OF INFLATION ON MY SAVINGS?"

In the late 1970s and early '80s, we were saddled with an inflation rate in the teens. Since the mid-'80s, however, the economy has prospered and our Federal Reserve Board has made inflation fighting its chief mission. As a result, inflation has averaged under 4 percent. "The inflation monster is caged and under control," some observers say. Other pundits, even more optimistic, declare that inflation is nearly dead.

Granted, 4 percent inflation sure beats the double digits. But we need to keep in mind that, even if we sustain a relatively modest inflation rate of 4 percent, the effect on our purchasing power in New Retirement can be dramatic. Not only will it affect the amount of income we'll need to draw when retirement begins, but it also will keep the cost of living moving skyward as we grow older. Consider what 4 percent inflation means when it comes to items that are part of our daily lives:

Figure 6.1

THE IMPACT OF 4 PERCENT INFLATION

PURCHASE	TODAY'S PRICE	IN 25 YEARS	IN 35 YEARS	IN 45 YEARS
Gallon of gas	$1.25	$3.33	$4.93	$7.30
Cup of coffee	$3.00	$8.00	$11.84	$17.52
Box of cereal	$3.95	$10.53	$15.59	$23.07
Movie ticket	$8.00	$21.33	$31.57	$46.73
Pair of jeans	$40.00	$106.63	$157.84	$233.65
Coach airfare	$267.00	$711.78	$1,053.61	$1,559.59
Med.-class car	$20,000.00	$53,316.73	$78,921.78	$116,823.51

Seventeen dollars and fifty-two cents for a cup of coffee? Yes, even at only 4 percent, inflation can seriously affect our purchasing power over time. This is why our pre-Commencement goal for average return on investment is 10 percent per year or more, and at least 8 percent during New Retirement. We can't stay ahead of inflation by parking all of our money in "safe" investments earning just 4 to 6 percent per year.

But dwelling on inflation is like dwelling on Blitzkrieg Murphy: It hurts just to think about it. If the past is any indication, it's likely that returns on most growth and growth-and-income investments will continue to increase at a pace that keeps you ahead of the game. There are no guarantees, of course, and I share the financial industry's disclaimer that "past performance is no guarantee of future results." What the past *does* tell us is that as long as we invest for growth, we have a good chance of staying ahead of inflation over the long term, especially if we revisit and adjust our projections every year or two in view of how the economy is behaving at the time.

"SHOULD I WAIT TILL I'VE PAID ALL MY DEBTS?"

An excellent question, since debt is one of our greatest hindrances to financial freedom. And, as with the challenge of building a contingency fund, financial counselors differ on whether we should postpone long-term savings to first get totally free of consumer debt. There's no question that one of the best, sure-thing investments around is paying off your credit cards; if your card charges 16.9 percent interest and you pay your balance in full, you've virtually gained 16.9 percent on your "investment" in the form of interest you won't have to pay. And the timeless wisdom of the Scriptures advises that clearing debt is essential to financial freedom:

> The borrower is servant to the lender. . . . Do not be a man who strikes hands in pledge or puts up security for debts; if you lack the means to pay, your very bed will be snatched from under you. (Proverbs 22:7, 26–27)

But as we have seen, the Scriptures also counsel us to set aside what we can for the future. It's a genuine dilemma. And human nature adds another wrinkle: Say you decide to postpone New Retirement savings until you're free and clear of all consumer debt. But as you're working off the debt, along comes a big Murph, and you finance it with your credit card instead of cash. If it's not a Murph, it's a dinner out or an impulse purchase or maybe even an innocent tank of gas for the SUV—any of which keeps your credit card balance(s) in that frustrating one-step-forward, one-step-back mode. As you struggle to make headway against the debt, months can pass. Perhaps years. Precious time in which you lose out considerably on the tax deductibility and tax-deferred compounding available in your 401(k) or IRA accounts.

By all means, if your heart tells you to devote every available dollar to getting out of debt, I can't argue with that. It's good citizenship and makes good financial sense. Just be passionate about paying off your debt as quickly as possible and, just as important, avoid taking on any new debt in the process. Chapter 9 will help you accomplish this worthwhile objective.

But if you feel you simply cannot afford to delay New Retirement savings any longer, then I believe it's also wise to get started now even as you work at eliminating your debt. Just as we suggested in building a contingency reserve, begin saving *something*—perhaps 2 or 3 percent of your salary—and then gradually increase the percentage to savings as you reduce your consumer debt. This method will require more time, of course, but it also provides a big emotional boost as you see progress in both arenas.

"WHAT IF I'M GETTING A LATE START?"

It could be that vacillating income, other priorities, Murphs, or procrastination has caused you to get a relatively late start in your financial preparation for seniority. The bad news, as you know, is that you have less time with which to build your Big Sum; in fact, you may even need to adjust it to a more realistic level. But the good news is that you've recognized the challenge and there are some smart moves you can make between now and Commencement Day.

❏ Make New Retirement savings your top financial priority and try to contribute the maximum legal amount to every tax-advantaged retirement plan available to you. (The "found money" ideas in chapter 4 should help; also pay extra attention to chapters 10 and 11.)

❏ Take on some extra work and direct your additional income to long-term savings.

❏ Plan on a later Commencement and continue working in order to further build your tax-deferred savings. Three to five years' additional contributions, combined with tax deductibility, tax deferral, equity investments, and compounding, can make a dramatic difference in your Big Sum. Working longer will also qualify you for more monthly Social Security income, if you want to plan on that.

❏ Consider working part-time *after* Commencement, whether in your present industry or in a totally new field. You wouldn't be alone. A recent study by the American Association of Retired Persons reveals that 80 percent of baby boomers plan to continue working during "retirement," whether full-time, part-time, or in a business of their own. Part-time work may, in fact, provide the best of both worlds: a more relaxed, flexible schedule and the continuing stimulation, productivity, and income of a job to do.

"SHOULDN'T I WAIT TILL MY KIDS ARE THROUGH COLLEGE?"

Paying for college boils down to four basic sources of funding: (1) what the institution itself might provide in the form of scholarships, grants, or financial aid; (2) what the government may provide

81

in the form of loans with favorable terms; (3) what your child can provide through his or her personal savings from work; and (4) what you can provide as parents.

Like our parents before us, all of us want our kids to enjoy a running start on their adult careers. And if that means college, most of us would prefer that our children begin their postgraduate careers without heavy student loans hanging over their heads. But college costs, and the typical family's ability to pay for them, have changed a tad since our own university days. In the early 2000s, a four-year public university education is projected to run approximately $40,000; private school could be more like $100,000. And these projections are tuition only—you also need to plan for room and board, books, and the usual incidentals of campus life.

So we face a dilemma: How much of our children's college education should we try to finance—and should we do so at the expense of our own retirement savings? I realize you may have some deep-seated personal priorities here, and I respect those convictions. So without being adamant, let me offer a perspective that more and more financial counselors seem to share regarding college for the kids, in the hope that you will find some guidance (and encouragement) for your own situation.

Keep in mind that the overall job environment for the next decades will place a higher premium on specific skills than on a general liberal arts education. Two examples of high-demand categories for the twenty-first century are computer-related specialties and healthcare, both of which will offer hundreds of subspecialties requiring technical training. Thus, depending on your child's strengths and interests, it could be that he or she would benefit more from a two-year technical training opportunity than from a traditional four-year college education.

PUT ON YOUR OWN MASK FIRST . . .

Whatever higher education opportunity your child pursues, financing it is likely to be a challenge unless dear, rich Aunt Lottie has offered to help. And while it may seem logical to cut back or postpone your own tax-deferred retirement savings in order to fund college for your kids, most financial planners advise against it; doing so could set back *your own* fiscal health to a point where both you and your college-educated children must struggle to provide in the future. You might liken this underlying principle to the instructions a flight attendant gives at the start of every commercial airline flight. You know the line . . . "In the unlikely event of a sudden loss of cabin pressure, adults should put on their oxygen masks *first, then* help young children with theirs." While this instruction may seem selfish, it's actually best for all involved: You won't be of much help to your children if you've already passed out. Therefore, adults should first make sure their own masks are on *in order to best help their children.*

In the same way, financial counselors advise, make sure your fiscal house is in order by making your own retirement savings your top financial priority. You've supported, nurtured, and provided for your children throughout their childhood and high-school years; you must now pay closer heed to your own future needs so that you won't be a financial drain on your children down the road.

PARTNERING WITH YOUR KIDS

In this light, more and more financial advisers advocate maintaining your tax-deferred retirement savings as top priority while partnering with your kids to share the costs of higher education. To do this, parents should discuss higher-education expectations with their children while kids are still in their mid-teens. In several loving but straightforward discussions, explore together what the child thinks he or she would like to pursue after high school. Be forthright about what you will and will not be able to do financially, perhaps spelling out the specific dollar amount or percentage of costs you will provide. Keeping expectations clear and realistic from the child's mid-teens will go a long way to prevent misunderstandings or ill feelings down the road.

WHERE SHOULD YOU SAVE FOR COLLEGE?

No-load (no sales commission) growth or growth-and-income mutual funds are great places to save for college. (Just be sure to keep these savings separate from your tax-advantaged retirement savings plans.) There is also a misnomered plan called an "Education IRA," which is not a retirement plan at all but allows you to set aside up to $500 per year for your child's college education. Contributions to Education IRAs are not tax-deductible, but earnings are completely tax-free if they are indeed used for education (at last report, not if used for a new speedboat). Any of the mutual fund families suggested in chapter 11 can provide more information.

Many parents believe that higher education is much more meaningful when children help pay for it, so they encourage their children from their middle-school years to work summer jobs and save aggressively for college. The children may then continue working summers and/or part-time while in college to contribute as much as they can to their education. Meanwhile, the parents continue to first address their top financial priority of saving for New Retirement in tax-advantaged savings plans, then set aside what they can to help with their children's college education.

PAYING YOUR PORTION

For your portion of college expenses, first try drawing from your current monthly cash flow if at all possible, then from any savings you've earmarked especially for college. Your next option is to borrow the remaining money you may need, keeping in mind that higher education for your child is most likely an *appreciating asset* (i.e., investing in his or her higher earning power) and thus a "good" debt instead of a consumer debt. (If you've seen the movie *Animal House*, or remember clearly your own college days, you may justifiably question this premise.) *Do not* tap your tax-advantaged retirement savings plans for this purpose, even though many offer borrowing privileges for college. You want to keep all New Retirement accounts separate and growing.

RAISING MONEY FOR COLLEGE

◇ Call 800-4FED-AID for the free government booklet, *The Student Guide: Financial Aid from the U.S. Department of Education.* Also see the Web site: http://www.ed.gov.

◇ Check http://finaid.org for a helpful potpourri of information regarding financial aid. It includes scholarship sources, advice from experts, even links to college-aid agencies.

◇ Buy the *College Costs and Financial Aid Handbook* at your bookstore or by calling College Board Publications, 800-323-7155.

◇ If you must borrow, consider a home-equity loan or home-equity line of credit. In most cases, interest on these loans will be tax-deductible.

◇ Ask about Federal Stafford Loans, available at your bank, savings and loan, or the college itself. These are made directly to the child but may be worth applying for because of favorable interest rates and payback terms.

◇ Call the College Board, 800-874-9390, and The Education Resources Institute, 800-255-8374—among the nation's leading private education lenders. Both offer favorable rates and payback terms.

◇ Forget withdrawing or borrowing from your tax-deferred retirement savings plans—too many strings attached and too much time-value lost. Keep these accounts separate, intact, and growing for your future.

The bottom-line principle in all this is that you'll do what's best for both you *and* your children if you first put on your own oxygen mask, then help your children with theirs. In other words, keep your own tax-deferred savings plans your top priority for the long-term fiscal health of both you and your children. That done, *then* do what you can to assist your children in their higher education, even if it means borrowing some of the needed funds.

"WHAT IF I'LL HAVE DEPENDENT PARENTS?"

The answer to this question is much more distinct, especially for all who respect the teaching of the Scriptures: "If anyone does not provide for his relatives, and especially for his immediate family, he has denied the faith and is worse than an unbeliever" (1 Timothy 5:8).

This is not like the dilemma of whether to pay in full for your children's college education. Your children are at the beginning of their earning years; your parents are at the end of theirs. College is a good thing for the kids if you can swing it; food, lodging, and clothing are basic necessities for your parents. Your children have a whole world of choices before them; your parents' choices may be growing more limited each day.

There should be no question, no doubt. If we have aging parents who need our financial help, they should know we're here for them. They may not like the idea much, and it may be all they can do to accept our welcome, but our arms should be open wide. They gave so much of themselves—instilled in us their sense of citizenship, character, and values—and put their own dreams on hold to see us to adulthood. It's a debt we'll never be able to repay. But we can try by doing all we can to help fill their last decades with love, respect, involvement, and personal dignity. It may not be easy for us financially and may even cause us to postpone some of *our* dreams for a while, but it's the right thing to do. A couple of helpful steps to consider . . .

LOOK INTO LONG-TERM CARE INSURANCE

Almost 40 percent of Americans over sixty-five will spend some time in a nursing home. The average stay is just under three years—almost three times that for Alzheimer's patients—at a cost of $3,500 or more per month. Regular health insurance doesn't cover extended nursing-home care. Medicare kicks in only about 2 percent of the cost of nursing homes, and Medicaid takes effect only when the patient is deemed destitute. Thus even a temporary nursing-home stay could severely reduce your parents' retirement nest egg and even consume their pension or Social Security income—resulting in a financial burden on you and your siblings.

Your folks don't want to be a burden on you, so it's in their best interest as well as yours to discuss long-term care insurance (LTC). LTC is designed to pay part or all of the cost of nursing-home and in-home care, thus helping protect your parents' savings from the ravages of a lengthy nursing-home stay. The older they are when they buy, the higher the premium, of course—but premiums are locked in from the date of purchase, so the earlier they buy LTC coverage, the better.

Your folks may need for you to do the research and groundwork for them. Provisions, rates, and medical underwriting standards vary from company to company, so it pays to shop around. Insurance brokers who represent multiple companies can do most of the legwork for you; contact Bisys Long-Term Care Marketing Group, 800-678-4582, and Long-Term Care Quote, 800-587-3279.

GIVE THEM THE DIGNITY OF HELPING WITH EXPENSES

If aging, dependent parents need to live with your family and your cash flow is tight, you may wish to talk with them about sharing part of their monthly Social Security pension to help with groceries and household expenses. But be sure they always keep enough to maintain a sense of independence. And do everything you can to help them feel involved, productive, creative, and useful within the family.

MAKE THE MOST OF YOUR MOMENTS

Of the dilemmas we've discussed, if there is anything worth cutting back or even delaying our own New Retirement savings for, it's this one—making sure our parents are loved, involved, and cared for. If you approach each day with a spirit of gratitude and of giving back, you can truly enjoy these precious times of reflecting together; of probing your parents for stories, memories, and experiences; of drawing out the wisdom that long life has taught them; of taking the opportunity to express your love and appreciation for all they have done and been. Your whole family can be enriched by such open sharing.

At the same time, you can look on such opportunities as your personal reminder that you would prefer not to be financially dependent on *your own* adult children someday. As you provide loving assistance to dependent parents, rededicate yourself to arriving at your own Commencement Day with financial independence in hand—free of dependence on your children, on government, on charity. Free to pursue dreams, to step up, to give back. Free to truly make the most of the rest of your life.

Part One has demonstrated that you can.

Part Two will show you how.

PART TWO

THE SEVEN PILLARS OF FINANCIALLY INDEPENDENT RETIREMENT

7. SAY A HEARTY "THANKS"
THE FIRST PILLAR: AN ATTITUDE OF GRATITUDE

8. TAKE CARE OF THE TEMPLE
THE SECOND PILLAR: A COMMITMENT TO HEALTH AND VITALITY

9. GO DEBTFREE
THE THIRD PILLAR: FREEDOM FROM DEBT

10. PAY YOURSELF FIRST, AUTOMATICALLY
THE FOURTH PILLAR: DISCIPLINED, TAX-ADVANTAGED SAVINGS

11. PUT YOUR SAVINGS TO WORK
THE FIFTH PILLAR: INVESTING FOR GROWTH

12. PROTECT WHAT YOU'VE BUILT
THE SIXTH PILLAR: ASSET PROTECTION

13. MAKE YOUR MONEY LAST AS LONG AS YOU DO
THE SEVENTH PILLAR: AN INCOME YOU WON'T OUTLIVE

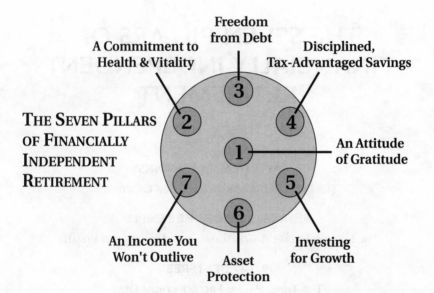

Freedom
from Debt

A Commitment to
Health & Vitality

Disciplined,
Tax-Advantaged Savings

THE SEVEN PILLARS
OF FINANCIALLY
INDEPENDENT
RETIREMENT

An Attitude
of Gratitude

An Income You
Won't Outlive

Asset
Protection

Investing
for Growth

SEVEN

SAY A HEARTY "THANKS"

The First Pillar: *An Attitude of Gratitude*

Some may think it odd that the first and central pillar of financial independence is an attitude of the heart. After all, what does gratitude have to do with building a financially independent retirement?

Frankly, I don't think financial freedom is possible without it.

Think back to one of your favorite Christmas stories . . . and a crotchety old London businessman who was filthy rich but spiritually destitute. Ebenezer Scrooge, who hoarded every crown, pound, and shilling, had more than enough for the rest of his days. But he wanted even more. Making money was his sole purpose. He couldn't even bring himself to spend a few pounds for sufficient heat in his office or to spiff up his bare-bones living quarters. And when a pair of solicitors approached him for a Christmas donation to the poor, Scrooge's first words were "Are there no prisons?"

He had made it all by himself and was indebted to no one. And he wasn't *about* to share with those who couldn't make it on their own.

WHAT THE DICKENS?

Are you starting to see why the attitude of one's heart is so important?

Ebenezer Scrooge was so rich he could have bought all of London, *but he was not financially free.* He had lost his perspective long ago, back when he chose wealth over the woman he loved. He became so focused on money that he totally forgot its rightful purpose and place in life—money became life itself. He was so proud of his acumen that he felt no sense of gratitude to Providence or anyone else for his fortune. In fact, when we meet Scrooge on that cold Christmas Eve, he is such an embittered old cuss that he can't think of a positive word for anybody—or about any aspect of his life. He's the quintessential miser—and he's miserable!

Until . . .

Until three nighttime visitors restore his perspective. You know the story. Ebenezer Scrooge learns that happiness has little to do with his portfolio but a lot to do with his perspective. That success is not a ledger filled with gigantic numbers but a life filled with generosity. That true wealth is realized only if we first realize our blessings. That the way to gain true riches is to first give some riches away.

Only when he learned to give back could he enjoy what he had gained.

Only when he was spiritually free could Scrooge also be financially free.

The old guy learned his lesson well. He found that without a grateful, generous heart, wealth means little and life means less. Christmas morn was the first time in decades he could exclaim, "I'm as happy as a schoolboy!" He wasted no time making up for lost time. His life became one of gratitude, outreach, and giving. He made the most of what he had . . . and made the most of the rest of his life!

THE MOST CRUCIAL PILLAR

Besides being a delightful Christmas story, Charles Dickens's tale illustrates the myopic misery that results from a life centered upon money. Granted, how we manage our money is important. But part of that stewardship is the realization that *money is not life—it is merely an implement of life.* To focus on money is not unlike focusing on a garden instrument instead of on the beautiful flowers a garden instrument helps produce. It cheats us of enjoying a bountiful harvest. It cheats the world of enjoying a beautiful, fragrant garden.

But Dickens also demonstrates, through Scrooge's conversion, how an *attitude of gratitude* can help us keep money in its proper perspective. Gratitude is a moment-by-moment spirit of thanksgiving. It's a humble acknowledgment that without God's grace and blessing we would have nothing . . . in fact, we would *be* nothing. All we have is from God. Our families and our homes are from him. Our talent and skill and our ability to work are because of him. Any financial reserves we build for the future are because of his blessing of wisdom and provision.

So without gratitude at the center of our financial lives, we do ourselves and those around us a grave disservice. Absent gratitude, *it's only about money*—much as it was for ol' Ebenezer before his guests set him straight. And if it's only about money, we're not going to be very pleasant people. Get a load of a savvy prediction the apostle Paul wrote about people in our time:

> There will be terrible times in the last days. People will be lovers of themselves, lovers of money, boastful, proud, abusive, disobedient to their parents, ungrateful, . . . without love, unforgiving, slanderous, without self-control, . . . treacherous, rash, conceited, lovers of pleasure rather than lovers of God. (2 Timothy 3:1–4)

Sounds like a really fun crowd, doesn't it? *Lovers of money, proud, ungrateful, without self-control, conceited*—really makes me want to hang out with this bunch. But as I write this, I find something strange happening. When I point an accusing finger at these ugly, ungrateful people Paul describes, I find three fingers pointing straight back at *me*. Without the spirit of God at work in my heart, I can be just as proud, just as ungrateful, just as conceited. Without gratitude to God, I can lose my perspective and become

93

a lover of money. I, too, can become stupidly obsessed with the garden implements instead of relishing the beautiful, fragrant flowers they help produce. If I don't have sincere love and thankfulness for God at the core of my being, you won't want to hang around *me,* either!

So let's be sure we keep money in its proper place. It's not life; it's merely an implement to help us live and enjoy life. Our relationship with the Creator, our spouses and children, our extended family and friends, our outreach to others, our personal growth, our health and well-being—those are the real priorities, the true riches of life. They're the fragrant, beautiful flowers that bring us joy.

Thus a sincere attitude of gratitude richly deserves its spot at the center of our discussion of personal finance. It's our central pillar; without it the others don't mean much. Heartfelt gratitude will go a long way toward helping us keep the right perspective toward money and, as a result, enjoy even more blessings down the road.

GAINING A HEART OF GRATITUDE

Alan D. Wright's wonderful book, *The God Moment Principle* (Multnomah, 1999), beautifully illustrates the importance of recognizing and expressing gratitude for the "God Moments" of life—moments of his provision, protection, healing, or guidance at a juncture in life's road. Alan recalls how his mother, at the end of each day, required him and his siblings to recount *two blessings* God had given them during the day. As you might imagine, the adolescent boys often whined at the requirement, and some of their recalled blessings weren't exactly mined from the theological depths. But as Alan grew into adulthood, he discovered that the discipline of gratitude had profoundly strengthened him. Gratitude made him more positive and optimistic. Gratitude made life more fun. Recalling the "God Moments" of his past gave him strength and assurance to face the trials of the future.

In fact, the attitude of gratitude imparted by Alan Wright's mother had such a lasting impact that today, Alan and his wife,

Anne, rarely fall asleep at night without first recalling for each other *two blessings* of their day.

So if the "dailiness" of life tends to get you down . . . if you're discouraged about the job, the marriage, the kids, or your personal place in it all . . . and even if your personal finances aren't looking real hot right now . . . set aside the despair and look for the blessings. They're there. Gratitude finds the good in the midst of the bad. Its horizon is always partly sunny, not partly cloudy. It gives you hope. It brings peace to your spirit, to your relationships, to your finances. It makes life fun . . . and makes you more fun to be around.

THE GRATITUDE JOURNAL

Let me share another "gratitude builder" that has meant a lot in my own life: the *gratitude journal*. It's simply a blank notebook in which I record thoughts and prayers of thanksgiving for the big and little blessings God brings my way. If I wake up in the morning and hear finches chattering outside my window, there are two blessings already: (1) I woke up, and (2) I enjoyed a marvelous concert by God's little creatures. In response, I might jot a sentence or two of praise for the new day. When God provides one of his miracles of direction, provision, or encouragement, I'll write a few notes about the situation and record my thanks for the way he came through. Journaling helps me orient my mind and emotions toward the good things. It makes my glass half-full instead of half-empty. It tunes my soul to "How Great Thou Art" instead of to how tough life is. It helps me give credit where credit is due.

Whenever real life seems to scream negativity from all directions, the gratitude journal helps me find and focus on the positives. It helps me realize that *God indeed cares*. If I'm struggling for direction, it reminds me of similar times in my past when God came through, and it fills me with faith that he'll do so again.

Why not try a gratitude journal for the next thirty days—and see what a difference it makes in your outlook? You may find, as many people do, that it's worth continuing for life.

GIVING: GRATITUDE IN WORK CLOTHES

Although gratitude is a dynamic quality in and of itself, its rewards don't stop there. When you're deeply appreciative of your blessings, when you're truly humbled by the way God provides for you, your gratitude is going to roll up its sleeves and go into action. It's going to put on its work clothes and look for ways to share with others.

And, paradoxically, here's where God comes through with even more blessings.

When you give, you do it to bless the receiver, right? You give to help meet a need, to show you care, to help point the receiver to the benevolence of God. Ironically, your act of giving blesses *you*, too—perhaps even more than it does the receiver. It's a paradox, but it's true: It is more blessed to give than to receive. You bless others; God blesses you. Here's how Jesus put it during his visit to Planet Earth:

> Give, and it will be given to you. A good measure, pressed down, shaken together and running over, will be poured into your lap. For with the measure you use, it will be measured to you. (Luke 6:38)

The Master often used imagery from real life to illustrate his point. Imagine, Jesus says, that you've just given someone a generous portion of grain from your supply. Will your generosity bare your cupboards? Cause your family to go hungry? Absolutely not. Out of gratitude to God, you've shared your provision with someone else. As the large, empty basket sits in your lap, God approaches with a huge, bottomless sack of fresh grain and begins replenishing your basket. You press the grain down to fill all the nooks and crannies. You shake it to settle the grain and make more room, and the blessings keep pouring in—to the point of overflowing. What you have given away, God has replenished—and then some. You now have what you need for today, something to set aside for tomorrow, and more to give to others—*a good measure, pressed down, shaken together, and running over.*

Giving is sharing the blessings of God. It is the visible manifestation of the honor we give him in our lives, of our gratitude for his provision, and of our obedience to his commands to share his love and care for those who are less fortunate. Because giving helps us keep money in perspective, it is essential to financial independence. God doesn't need our money, but he knows we need to give.

Have you discovered the joy of putting your gratitude in work clothes? Let me share some suggestions that will help you keep gratitude and giving where they belong: at the center of your financial life.

GIVE IN THE FIRST PLACE

On your list of monthly bills and other financial priorities, where do you place the act of giving?

For too many of us, giving is more of an afterthought than a priority. Some limit giving to occasional discards for the Salvation Army or a few dollars tossed into a red kettle at Christmas. Others share a bit here and there from the remainder of their income, if there is any.

But we're human; we know how money trickles through our fingers. If we relegate giving to the realm of afterthought, then it will happen only on those rare occasions when we feel we have plenty left over after paying for monthly needs and greeds. (How often, really, do we feel we have "plenty left over"?) Therefore, the key to successful giving is to turn the pattern around—to make giving our top spiritual and financial priority. King Solomon affirmed the wisdom of top-priority giving when he wrote, "Honor the LORD from your wealth, and from the *first* of all your produce" (Proverbs 3:9, NASB, emphasis added). To experience the true joy and blessing of giving, we may need to realign our spending priorities to make sure we give in the first place.

A MATTER OF PERSPECTIVE

"Funny how a dollar can look so big when you take it to church, and so small when you take it to the store."

—FRANK A. CLARK
Register and Tribune Syndicate, October 1970

GIVE CHEERFULLY

According to the Scriptures, God wants our giving to be a voluntary, cheerful, delightful act: "Each man should give what he has decided in his heart to give, not reluctantly or under compulsion, for *God loves a cheerful giver*" (2 Corinthians 9:7, emphasis added).

When you stop to think about it, giving cheerfully is simply the natural outflow of a spirit of gratitude. When we give from a happy heart, we're saying how grateful we are for all God has given us. If we smile as we give, so does he!

GIVE FAITHFULLY

Perhaps the best way to make giving a priority is through a *tithe*. The concept originated in Old Testament times, when loyal devotees of God honored him by giving the first one-tenth of their produce or income. To this day the tithe remains a basic guideline for charitable giving both in religious and secular circles. Many like to give even more than that, enjoying the calm assurance that God will always be faithful in meeting their needs.

If you have discovered the delight of giving money away, you already know something of the joy I've been talking about. But if giving faithfully from an attitude of gratitude is new to you, I want to encourage you to make it a nonoptional part of your financial and spiritual journey. At first you may wonder how you can give off the top and meet your other obligations. Trust me; you can do it. Give first, and soon your budget will reshape itself around your new priority. Determine the percentage of each month's income you want to give to your church and your favorite charitable organization(s). When payday comes, write these check(s) first, not last, to confirm the new importance of giving in your life.

GIVE WISELY

When considering investments for your Never Retire nest egg, it would be foolish to simply cast your savings dollars at the "opportunities" with the loudest, hardest sales pitches. You're going to invest thoughtfully and deliberately to enhance your chances of positive results.

Likewise, giving is the most important investment you'll ever make—and of course you want your investments to yield good results. As you contemplate to whom you should direct your gifts of time, talent, and treasure, it's no time to be careless or hasty.

A few Christmases ago I received a phone call from a "police auxiliary" organization raising funds to support "our men behind the badge." I didn't want to be an Ebenezer Scrooge, but Kathy and I had agreed years before that we will never give or buy over the phone unless the call is from an entity we already know and support. I told the gentleman caller of our rule but assured him I'd be happy to review any literature he could send. We never received anything. Sure enough, a few weeks later our local newspaper announced that a fraudulent Christmas charity had been calling people to solicit money "on behalf of the local police."

Other charities may not be fraudulent, but they may mismanage donations to the point where a large percentage of each dollar is eaten up by "administration" costs. You may want to consult *Money* magazine's annual report on charitable organizations, which ranks each according to the percentage of each donor dollar that goes directly to front-line ministry.

If you're considering giving to an individual, take some extra precautions to be sure that he or she is in sincere need. I remember a single guy in his late-twenties who hinted that he was in dire financial straits. Initially I thought I might like to help him out. But further questioning revealed that, while he indeed had a cash flow problem, he was holding onto his multipremium cable TV service, continuing to dine out more often than not, and racking up untold credit card balances to purchase just about anything his little ol' heart desired. He also preferred staying in front of the TV on weekends over seeking supplemental income. I might have been more than happy to financially assist this gentleman with his needs, but I didn't feel led to help him maintain his greeds. I concluded that my giving might be better invested elsewhere.

GIVE QUIETLY

The ultimate purpose of giving is to glorify God, not ourselves. Yet our Creator knows us so well. He knows that, because we are self-centered, our giving may sometimes be selfishly motivated. But think about it from *his* perspective for a moment: If we announce our donation of time or money to such and such a cause, then it isn't a gift, it's public relations. If we manipulate our giving so we get the credit, it isn't a gift, it's self-glorification. We may as well emulate Hollywood and produce an endless string of shallow, self-congratulatory awards shows. We may as well erect a monument that reads, "To me, without whom this donation would not have been possible."

As a matter of fact, God doesn't seem to appreciate sanctimonious giving one bit. Please read carefully Jesus' words:

> Be careful not to do your "acts of righteousness" before men, to be seen by them. If you do, you will have no reward from your Father in heaven. So when you give to the needy, do not announce it with trumpets, as the hypocrites do in the synagogues and on the streets, to be honored by men. I tell you the truth, they have received their reward in full. But when you give to the needy, do not let your left hand know what your right hand is doing, so that your giving may be in secret. Then your Father, who sees what is done in secret, will reward you. (Matthew 6:1–4)

Doesn't beat around the bush, does he? When we announce our giving, we're actually being more boorish then blessful. We dishonor God, we cheapen the dignity of the recipient, and we don't do ourselves a whole lot of good either. Giving in secret may be contrary to human nature, but then so is most of divine wisdom. God wants us to give quietly and from a thankful, humble heart that longs to bring honor and glory to his name. Giving quietly is vital to honoring him and to receiving his blessing in return.

May your heart be filled with gratitude today and every day. Look for God's blessings and remember them, for they will buttress your faith and your confidence for whatever the future holds. Live each moment in awe of his goodness and in humble thanksgiving that he truly, truly wants what's best for you.

There isn't a better way to keep your finances in perspective, no better way to fuel your journey to financial independence. An attitude of gratitude will spill over into unselfish giving. Your giving will bless you spiritually, relationally, emotionally, financially, and—just as the Master promises—abundantly.

Like a good measure, pressed down, shaken together, and running over.

ACTION POINTS

Throughout *Never Retire* we've provided Action Points pages to help you personalize and apply what you're reading. Use these pages to record key steps you feel led to take in preparation for New Retirement.

HABITS I WANT TO CHANGE

-
-
-
-

NEW ATTITUDES I WANT TO LIVE BY

-
-
-
-

ACTION STEPS I NEED TO TAKE

1.
2.
3.
4.
5.

EIGHT

I

TAKE CARE OF THE TEMPLE

The Second Pillar: *A Commitment to Health and Vitality*

Whoever thinks golf is sedentary has never golfed with me. I get more exercise than just about any other golfer on the course. That's because I usually play three fairways at once, which means I can turn a simple 397-yard hole into a 900-yarder.

For some reason, those who golf with me or behind me don't seem to appreciate my skills as much as I do. The other day, as I contemplated a shot, I asked a friend if he thought a six iron would get me to the green.

"Which green?" he asked.

"The one straight ahead. Will a six iron get me there?"

"Eventually," he said.

I think he may be jealous because I pack a lot more golf into eighteen holes than he does. All that walking and whacking keeps me in good shape. I enjoy the game and hope to keep playing until the Lord takes me to the big course in the sky. My golf buddies assure me they're praying that my dream will come true.

I've learned a lot about the game since I started. My first couple of years I thought I was doing great until someone told me it's the low score that wins. I then paid for a private lesson in which the golf pro suggested I try some clubs other than the putter. I must be a fast learner because that single bit of advice shaved a hundred strokes off my score. In the years since, I often see other golfers shake their heads in amazement as they watch me, so clearly my lesson was worth every dime.

SOME MUCH-NEEDED R & R

I took up golf for a new challenge, and that it has been. But it also provides some good exercise and gives me a mental break from the pressures of the day. I don't take the game so seriously that it makes me mad. The Lord has even kept me from thinking or saying naughty words. (I do find myself saying "rats" a lot, but I figure he doesn't mind if I take a rodent's name in vain.) If I ever take the game so seriously that it makes me angry and frustrated, I'll give it a break. After all, I'm there to relax, rejuvenate, and enjoy.

To my knowledge—and I've scoured all the ancient texts for this—they didn't have golf in Jesus' day. I didn't come across anything about tennis or fitness clubs either. Regardless, it's fascinating to note that, even as Jesus Christ was changing the course of history in just three short years, he knew the importance of breaking away from his busy schedule for much-needed R & R. We're told that he often rose early in the morning, while it was still dark, and went away by himself to pray. On another occasion, the Lord saw that his disciples were both stressed out and pooped out from the hectic pace they'd been keeping. Read the prescription he gave them:

> Then, because so many people were coming and going that [the disciples] did not even have a chance to eat, he said to them, "Come with me by yourselves to a quiet place and get some rest." So they went away by themselves in a boat to a solitary place. (Mark 6:31–32)

If golf had been invented back then, I have a feeling at least a few of the disciples would have headed to the links. Instead, they took a cruise—not a cushy *Love Boat* cruise but a fishing boat cruise that had them hoisting and trimming sail, riding waves, feeling sun and wind in their faces, breathing fresh air. Even in the midst of Kingdom business, the Master knew the importance of R & R to the human mind, body, and spirit.

Centuries later, Vance Havner took Jesus' example to heart when he said, "If you don't come apart . . . you *will* come apart." Medical studies consistently confirm the wisdom of the Lord's example: Breaking away from routine for rest and activity unrelated to work will make us healthier and more effective when we return to those routines. "Coming apart" is time well invested because it adds days to our life and life to our days.

THE PHYSICAL-FISCAL CONNECTION

Getting away for rest is a key component of our second pillar of financially independent retirement: *a commitment to health and vitality*. Now I realize that some good readers may question the connection between health and financial freedom, so let me share four reasons why we're discussing health and vitality here:

- Good health keeps the mind and body fresh, alert, and strong. A sound mind and strong body help you do your job well. When you do your job well, you earn the money to save and invest for your future.

- Good health helps you avoid huge, asset-draining medical expenses now and down the road.

- Good health will also help supply the energy and vitality you will want in order to enjoy the active, fully engaged life style of New Retirement. Your commitment to health and vitality will help you thrive.

- And the bonus: Health and vitality make you feel good. Physically, mentally, emotionally, and spiritually, you feel more alive. Upbeat. Energetic. Ready to eat problems for breakfast. Please understand, I don't contend that feeling good is essential to a fulfilling life because there are countless people who accomplish wonders despite chronic pain, disability, and ill health. But when you think about it, these amazing people rise above their limitations because they make the most of what they do have. They radiate vitality because vitality is really an attitude of mind and soul, a conscious decision to regard life positively and enthusiastically regardless of how they may feel physically. We would all do well to emulate them.

I'm not a doctor, nor do I play one on TV. Neither am I a physiologist or nutritionist. But as a personal finance specialist who believes there's a definite connection between physical fitness and fiscal fitness, I would be remiss if we did not devote at least a few moments to this important topic. In fact, we'll keep it brief by limiting our discussion to a quick 'n' easy "Top Ten List" for health and vitality—the essentials we might all want to keep in mind to help us make the most of midlife, pre-retirement, and New Retirement.

TOP TEN HABITS FOR HEALTH AND VITALITY

1. Go to sleep. That's right, it starts with sleep. A decade ago scientists pooh-poohed the age-old advice that we need eight hours' sleep each night. However, recent multiple studies have concluded that Ma and Grandma were right: Most of us do need at least eight hours, and we're not getting it. In fact, we're a sleep-deprived society, which goes a long way toward explaining sleepiness, crankiness, exhaustion, susceptibility to illness, depression, road rage, and how some politicians get elected. Sound sleep—at least eight hours' worth—seems to be foundational to sound health.

2. Give yourself a break. Give yourself frequent minibreaks during the day to decompress. If possible, get away from your work station; shift your mind into neutral; do some deep breathing; and stretch to loosen neck, shoulder, and back muscles. You'll feel refreshed after just a couple of minutes. Try, too, to take at least one longer break at midday for a brief, vigorous walk. Don't let yourself think about work—use the time to watch people in the park, to enjoy God's creation, or perhaps to pray for friends and family.

3. Enjoy these healthy foods as often as you can. Studies show the following foods to be especially effective in supplying your body and brain with the nutrients they need for strength and efficiency— while helping prevent problems such as cancer, heart attack, diabetes, and stroke: fresh fruits, fresh vegetables, whole grains, olive oil, nuts, salmon and tuna, and green and black tea.

4. Cut back on (or cease) some unhealthy habits. Do you smoke? Over-imbibe alcohol, coffee, soft drinks? Stay up too late at night? Overdo high-fat foods and snacks? Eat too much chocolate? (I realize that for some of us there's no such thing as "too much chocolate," but I must be fair.) Pick one unhealthy habit that you'd like to change—just one for now—and dedicate yourself to making the change permanent. You can do it!

5. Laugh. Ah, the incredible, cleansing, soothing power of laughter. Several years back, author Norman Cousins set the medical establishment on its ear when he documented how, after doctors gave him little hope of overcoming his debilitating disease, he found healing in laughter. In the face of agony, he watched movie after movie of the Marx Brothers, Laurel and Hardy, and other classic comedies—and he laughed. Laughed so much that his body hurt less . . . and less . . . and he regained his functionality for several more years.

We now know that, inside Cousins's body, his laughter was releasing powerful endorphins to strengthen both mind and body. If endorphins are that strong against actual illness and agony, imagine what they can do to help strengthen and rejuvenate us for the stresses of our own daily lives. All we need to do is laugh and let them do their job.

Laughter's a big part of this thing we call vitality. It helps keep both the body and the spirit upbeat. Look for the humor, then let 'er rip!

6. Supplement your nutrition. The consensus among nutritionists is that in today's high-stress, high-pollution world, good foods alone fall short of providing the quantity and balance of vitamins, minerals, and other nutrients we need. So it makes good sense to supplement our food intake each day with a high-potency multivitamin and mineral formula. As we grow older, we'll want to pay special attention to our intake of calcium for bone density and to vitamins C, E, and beta carotene for their antioxidant benefits. There's also a lot of encouraging news regarding the effectiveness of certain herbal supplements, among them Ginkgo biloba for enhanced mental alertness; St. John's wort for emotional stability; and phytoestrogen, a kinder, gentler hormone replacement therapy for women in midlife. You may find it worthwhile to consult a nutritionist about your particular life style and needs, as Kathy and I have done.

7. *Get away from it all—soon and often.* A psychologist friend of mine contends that America is centuries behind Europe and other parts of the world when it comes to vacations and holidays. They take six to eight weeks; we take one to three. When life gets tough, they break away and relax; we work harder. We may not be able to change the vacation policy at our places of employment, but we can take full advantage of whatever vacation time we do have. Don't feel the slightest smidgen of guilt about taking every moment you're entitled to. You've more than earned it. Get away from it all, enjoy your family and the world outside your window, and inhale the blessing of rejuvenation. Jesus' example, of course, was right on the money: Breaking away to rest is time well invested.

8. *Exercise.* A brisk thirty-minute walk, jog, bike ride, or aerobic workout at least three days a week for the cardiovascular system. A moderate resistance workout (dumbbells, barbells, or weight machines) a minimum of three days each week for muscle tone and strength. Find a routine you like, do it faithfully for three straight weeks, and you'll be hooked—it's called "positive addiction." Aerobic and resistance training are both essential for your physical health. They also work wonders for your morale!

9. *Make water your favorite beverage.* Lots of it. At least eight 8-ounce glasses a day. More before, during, and after exercise. Sheri Rose Shepherd's *Eating for Excellence Cookbook* (Multnomah,

1999) states the reason well: "Water puts oxygen into your blood and the blood brings oxygen to your brain. It cleans out your colon, flushes out fat, relieves water retention, creates beautiful skin, gives you more energy, removes toxins from your body, and is essential to your health."

10. Cover yourself. I recently saw a very effective poster issued by the American Cancer Society. It showed a daredevil rock climber hanging one-handed from an overhang thousands of feet above the ground—and with no safety rope. The caption read: *Can you believe this maniac? No sunscreen.*

Ask any dermatologist and he or she will confirm that instances of skin cancer, especially the killers such as malignant melanoma, are increasing at an alarming rate worldwide. Those tans we thought were so cool-looking when we were kids are now proving lethal. Now there's no such thing as a healthy suntan.

I must admit I'm a bit biased here: My dad was one of melanoma's many victims. It's not a pleasant way to die, but Dad did so bravely and with dignity. If you're going to spend time outside, especially during the sun's peak hours from 10 A.M. to 3 P.M., do yourself and your loved ones a big favor: Cover as much skin as possible. What you can't cover, use a sunscreen of SPF 30 or higher.

MAKE YOUR M.D. YOUR TEAMMATE

No one really enjoys the sundry pokes and prods that go with visits to the doctor, but those regular physical exams are essential to the stewardship of our health, especially as we grow older. If your physician spots a potential problem, he or she can check it out further and, if necessary, administer treatment. If you're pronounced healthy, you'll gain an extra shot of confidence and peace of mind.

Most doctors recommend a physical exam at least every two years through our forties, then once each year thereafter. You probably will need to take the initiative to schedule your physicals because, unlike dentists, auto mechanics, and life-insurance salesmen, M.D.s generally don't send reminders. But it's initiative worth taking. Put your own reminders in your long-range planning calendar and call faithfully for appointments. Make your doctor a teammate in your commitment to health and vitality. An ounce of prevention today will help you avoid expensive, debilitating problems later.

IT MUST BE IN CASE OF HAIL . . .

Our first and central pillar of financially independent retirement was *an attitude of gratitude*—an upbeat spirit of joy and thanksgiving for the blessings God brings into our lives. The second pillar, *a commitment to health and vitality*, reminded us that being good stewards of our health *today* plays a big role in the quality of life we hope to enjoy after Commencement Day. Now we move on to solving a much-too-common problem: consumer debt.

Want to get out of debt—for good? Free up more money for your New Retirement savings program? We're going to do just that in the next chapter. I must say good-bye for now because my golf partners have just pulled into the driveway. I'm not sure why, but they're all wearing hard hats.

You Know You're Getting Older When . . .

As we journey through midlife and pre-retirement, bodily changes are inevitable. So's gravity. One of the secrets to vitality is to do whatever you can to stay physically and mentally healthy, then relax and laugh about the rest. I find myself laughing a lot more lately.

In that spirit, I enjoy collecting "You Know You're Getting Older" tidbits, even if a few strike a little too close to home. Here are several I've accumulated over the years.

You Know You're Getting Older When . . .
- your broad mind and narrow waist trade places
- you look forward to a dull evening
- you turn out the light for economic reasons rather than romantic ones
- you sit in a rocking chair and can't get it going
- you feel drawn to cafeterias like a horse to water
- your knees buckle and your belt won't
- you catch yourself driving below the speed limit
- you're 17 around the neck, 42 around the waist, and 96 around the golf course
- you just can't stand people who are intolerant
- you burn the midnight oil until 9 P.M.
- your pacemaker raises the garage door when you see a pretty girl go by
- the little gray-haired lady you help across the street is your wife
- dialing long distance wears you out
- you bound out of bed each morning at the crack of 9:30
- you feel like the morning after but you didn't go anywhere the night before
- you get winded playing checkers
- your children begin to look middle-aged
- you know all the answers but nobody asks you the questions

ACTION POINTS

Throughout *Never Retire* we've provided Action Points pages to help you personalize and apply what you're reading. Use these pages to record key steps you feel led to take in preparation for New Retirement.

HABITS I WANT TO CHANGE

-
-
-
-

NEW ATTITUDES I WANT TO LIVE BY

-
-
-
-

ACTION STEPS I NEED TO TAKE

1.
2.
3.
4.
5.

NINE

GO DEBTFREE

The Third Pillar: *Freedom from Debt*

Gary and Rachel sat across from me, their financial papers scattered before them. "I think we got ourselves in too deep," Gary observed as he shoved a stack of credit card statements toward me.

Both in their early forties, Gary and Rachel had asked for an appointment following a personal finance seminar. Together they enjoyed an income of more than $75,000, but they were frustrated at their tight cash flow each month and the fact that they had little left over to save and invest for their future. As we came to their consumer-debt situation, Gary had offered his insight before I even had a chance to ask: "We got ourselves in too deep. Our debts are killing us."

He was stating the obvious. In addition to their mortgage and a loan on one of their three cars, this otherwise bright couple had accumulated debts of more than $14,000 on several credit cards.

"Tell me about your credit card habits," I prodded.

"Well, it seems like everyone wants to give us credit," Rachel began. "We get new card offers almost every week, and we thought it would be smart to build up as much of a credit line as possible in case of an emergency. Our intentions were good, but I think the temptation was too much."

Gary picked up the beat from there. "First it was a $2,500 computer system, which we thought was easy to justify with our work and all. Then we wanted some new furniture for the dining room and den, and the more we looked, the more eager we were to get it right away. So we put it on the cards, thinking we'd just bear down and pay it off within three or four months. But then we just kept using the cards."

"Clothes and other things for the kids, Christmas gifts . . ."

"Birthday gifts, our anniversary, vacations . . ."

The litany continued. Whenever they spotted something they wanted or needed, they pulled out a credit card. When they went out to dinner or Saturday brunch, they used a credit card. Their house and garage were full, but their bank account was nearly empty. Now it was wake-up time: Gary and Rachel were barely making ends meet. After paying their mortgage, utilities, groceries, car payment, and other nonoptional monthly expenses, they could barely make minimum payments on their credit card debt. As Rachel summarized, "We feel like we're barely making it from paycheck to paycheck, let alone saving anything for our future."

Unfortunately, Gary and Rachel are typical of the baby boomer generation. Studies reveal that 25 percent of Americans between the ages of thirty-five and fifty-four have not yet begun to save for their retirement years, and I believe the chief reason is our day-to-day spending habits. We tend to be self-indulgent. Unlike our parents' generation, we don't like to save for something before we buy it. "Wait" is not an active part of the boomer vocabulary. If we see it and think we need it, we think we need it *now.*

The average American family holds a credit card debt of more than $7,000 on seven to eight cards. If this is the *average,* untold multitudes like Gary and Rachel carry consumer debt far above that amount. The price? Well, Gary and Rachel's $14,000 credit card debt was compounding at an average of 18 percent annual interest. Their immediate price was more than $2,500 per year in interest payments alone. Their big-picture price was what we call *opportunity cost:* what they could have been earning on both the principal and interest had they been able to save and invest it instead of shoveling it toward debt repayment. At a time when they needed to be saving and investing aggressively for their retirement years, Gary and Rachel were in financial bondage to their creditors.

CREDIT'S EVIL TWIN

I'll admit that credit, when used with discernment, can be a very positive thing. Without credit most of us couldn't buy, and eventually own, our own home. Without credit the vast majority of businesses couldn't bridge their slow seasons or take advantage of the growing seasons. Credit often enables deserving students who otherwise couldn't attain their educational and professional objectives to earn college or postgraduate degrees. Credit can help us handle the financial impact of hefty medical expenses. And, although vehicles depreciate in value, many fine people would be without needed transportation if they did not have some form of credit. A person's "credit rating"—the cumulative, personal record of responsibility with available credit—is a key indicator of his or her financial strength and integrity.

But there's a catch. Like one character on every TV soap opera, credit has an evil twin—a cunning, greedy monster who masquerades as helpful while doing everything possible to pull good people down. The good twin helps us finance *appreciating or necessary assets* such as homes, businesses, education, medical treatment, and necessary transportation. The evil twin, consumer credit, encourages us to finance *depreciating and consumable items* such as meals out . . . appliances . . . makeup and designer fragrances . . . concert or theater tickets . . . clothes and shoes . . . computer systems . . . new CD and video systems . . . vacations . . . and more transportation than necessary. Why deprive yourself? Simply say "Charge it" and enjoy these things *now!*

Which is precisely how we get into trouble. Otherwise smart individuals and couples find themselves unable to enjoy the present and unable to save and invest for their future because they are paying out hundreds each month for items that are rapidly depreciating or were consumed long ago.

Do you, like the average family, carry credit card debt? You may not have as much debt as Gary and Rachel did; I hope not. But if you carry any credit card debt at all, you're making your financial life a lot tougher than necessary. You're *definitely* compromising your future independence by tying up today's dollars to pay for events that happened weeks, months, or even years ago.

"EASY CREDIT" IS AN OXYMORON

"Oh, but it's so convenient," the shills claim. "Why deprive yourself? You deserve that two-week cruise now! Our rates are low for the next six months. It makes good sense to use our card for everything you want—even cash advances to get ahead!"

Au contraire, evil twin. Consumer debt (borrowing for depreciating or consumable items) does not get you ahead; it sets you back. The truth is that "easy credit" and "convenient credit" are oxymorons—self-contradictory, like "a good cigarette." Sure, consumer credit may be easy or convenient to use, but it's neither easy nor convenient to service.

In fact, it makes little sense at all.

First, *borrowing on depreciating or consumable items pits the power of compounding against you.* When you charge purchases of appliances, clothing, tools, computers, meals out, vacations—anything that does not *appreciate in value* over time—you're robbing your future to pay for your past. You will pay 16, 18, 20 percent interest, sometimes spreading the payback over several years, while the item rapidly decreases in value. In the case of consumable goods, the depreciation is instantaneous—yet you're stuck paying for it over the course of several months.

Second, *servicing your debt prevents you from doing more positive things with your money, such as saving and investing for future needs and dreams.* When you carry consumer debt, your monthly income can become so tied up paying for depreciating or perished items that you are unable to build your own emergency reserve, save for planned expenditures, invest for your retirement years, or give to your church or favorite charity. To state it succinctly, consumer debt consumes income.

Third, *borrowing places you at a relational disadvantage as well as a financial one.* The ancient proverb speaks wisely for today: "The rich rule over the poor, *and the borrower is servant to the lender*" (Proverbs 22:7, emphasis added). When you owe, the lender calls the shots. He dictates minimum payment, interest charges, and due dates. He makes the profit; you take the loss. If the lender is someone you know personally, you may experience a degree of discomfort whenever you're in the same room, worshiping in the same church, or residing in the same town—the obligation constantly hovers between you. Being "servant to the lender" is no picnic, and it's definitely not financial freedom.

As you plan for New Retirement, you will find your progress dramatically hindered if you carry consumer debt. Likewise, if you can break free of the consumer-debt trap now, and stay free the rest of your days, you'll experience dynamic progress on your journey. That's why freedom from debt is one of our Seven Pillars of Financially Independent Retirement.

THE JOY OF BEING DEBTFREE

I like to take the term "debt free" and make one word of it: DEBTFREE. To me, this little wordplay helps convey a focused sense of excitement at the financial and emotional uplift you'll experience once you climb out of the consumer-debt quagmire. You won't just be debt free, you'll be DEBTFREE! (Feel the difference?)

When you become DEBTFREE, you'll discover several very special benefits.

√ *You're going to be in control of your cash flow.* When you no longer have to service those debilitating monthly credit card payments, you have more money to enjoy life, handle emergencies, make purchases on a paid-in-full basis, give to your church or favorite charity, build your savings reserve, and invest for future dreams.

√ *You will stop compound interest from working against you and get it working for you.* Instead of paying 16, 18, 20 percent on the money you owe, you'll be earning 5 to 20 percent (sometimes more) on those funds as you redirect them toward savings and investments. Eliminate the payout, add the earnings, and in effect you're earning 21 to 40 percent on those dollars!

√ *You'll be able to make future purchases with cash.* When there's a genuine need or you just want to do something fun, you'll pay with cash instead of plastic. With your rejuvenated savings program, the funds will be there for you, earmarked for just such an event. You won't spend months or years and countless interest dollars paying for your purchase. You'll be "in charge" instead of being charged by the lender.

√ *You will dramatically speed up your journey toward financial independence.* An average monthly credit card payment of $75 over the next twenty-five years robs you of $22,500 you could be saving and investing. However, with that debt paid off, you can contribute that $75 to tax-deferred investments where, at 10 percent, it can grow to more than $99,500 over the same twenty-five years. This is why you don't want to pay today for yesterday's indulgences—or pay tomorrow for today's. Becoming DEBTFREE will free up those debt-servicing dollars and turn them into YOU-servicing dollars.

√ *You will feel financially free.* This is perhaps the greatest benefit of all. No longer will you feel like an oppressed "slave to the lender," making endless payments on depreciating or already-consumed purchases. You'll enjoy the peace of mind that comes from staying current and paying as you go—and peace of mind is one of the best returns on investment you'll ever achieve.

NINE STEPS TO A DEBTFREE LIFE

I hope you're seeing that consumer debt only stacks the odds against you. And I hope you're as excited as I am about the financial and emotional progress you're going to experience as you turn those debilitating liabilities into powerful growth assets.

You may be thinking, *Sure, I want to pay off my debt. But not quite yet—we need a new car.* Or, *Sure, but after Christmas.* Or, *After vacation.* Believe me, I've heard every reason for putting off debt elimination—I used to come up with some good ones myself. Please don't procrastinate when it comes to this vital pillar of financial freedom. No consumable or depreciating purchase is worth the ravages of debt. Becoming DEBTFREE is one of the most positive, powerful moves you can make in your financial life. The sooner you do so, the more you'll have working in your favor.

Today is the day we begin to make it happen. Starting right now, follow these strategic steps to gain freedom from consumer debt— for good.

1. MAKE THE COMMITMENT: NO MORE CREDIT CARD DEBT

Decide now, boldly and irrevocably, that from this moment forward you will take on absolutely no more credit card debt. From this moment forward you will cease robbing your future to pay for your past. You will operate strictly on a cash-only, pay-as-you-go basis.

As you seek to live by this commitment, continue to think DEBTFREE. When temptation strikes (and it will, within approximately sixty seconds) think DEBTFREE. If you feel you need something now but would have to put it on credit, think DEBTFREE. It's your new resolution, your new way of life. You can do it, and you'll be glad you did.

POSSIBLE EXCEPTIONS TO THE NO-DEBT COMMITMENT

The only possible exceptions to your DEBTFREE commitment are (1) a mortgage on your home, which in most cases is an *appreciating* asset and thus not consumer debt; (2) financing, if necessary, to help you or your child attain higher education; (3) urgent or necessary medical care not covered by your health insurance; and (4) a loan for a necessary vehicle— definitely a *depreciating* asset but, realistically, an asset for which most people cannot plunk down payment-in-full.

√ If you take out a mortgage on your home, try to limit the mortgage to no more than three times your annual income—more than that puts you in bondage to your own house. Two and a half times or less is even better.

√ If your child is approaching college age and you don't have enough funds saved, hold a loving, honest planning session to lay out what you can contribute and what he or she will need to contribute. Then shop aggressively to make up the difference with scholarships, grants, and education loans.

√ Take advantage of special medical savings plans your company may provide, such as flexible spending accounts. These let you set aside a fixed sum from each paycheck, income tax–free, to apply to future medical expenses. There are catches, so read the fine print carefully—but these accounts will allow you to pay pretax dollars for most medical and dental charges your health insurance does not cover, including deductibles and copayments.

√ If you must finance a vehicle, limit financing to one vehicle at a time. Buy "almost new" instead of new to take advantage of early depreciation, and finance only after a concerted effort to negotiate the principal down as low as possible. (In the long run, you want to position yourself so you can pay cash for all future vehicles.)

Everything else in your life is going to be cash-only, pay-as-you-go. This means that *if you don't have the cash, you won't buy the product*—you're going to learn to wait, to save up, to temper your small-picture impulses with big-picture discipline.

2. REDUCE YOUR CARD COLLECTION TO ONE CARD

I realize this step is going to seem melodramatic. But let me assure you that if you can summon the courage to take this step and live by it, you'll be rewarded many times over. It requires you to confront the easy-credit, instant-gratification deceptions that have gotten good people into bad trouble. It challenges you to be a wise, forward-looking contrarian—to rise above the crowd and stand strong against the acquisitive life style that only impedes financial independence.

WHY MULTIPLE CARDS ARE A BAD IDEA

If you're like the average American family, you possess more than one credit card. Like Gary and Rachel, your intentions may have been innocent enough—to build a line of credit in case of a big emergency someday. But the truth is, you don't want or need much of this type of credit. Why? Two good reasons.

First, even if you've wisely kept those card balances at or near zero, the sum of your available credit may actually be held against you when it's time to apply for *good credit* such as a home mortgage, equity line of credit, or business loan. Mortgage lenders have to assume that you could max out every cent of credit that is available to you, which in turn would make it tougher for you to repay their loan.

Second, multiple cards are a bad idea because you simply don't need the motive or the means to accrue thousands of dollars in consumer debt. Your goal is to reduce temptation, not increase it—and the best way to reduce temptation is to reduce the number of opportunities to take on new debt.

Today, right now, you can gain a huge degree of control over your spending by reducing your number of credit cards to one. Here's what to do:

First, pull every credit card from your wallet: Visa, MasterCard, Discover, You-Name-It. Don't forget department store cards, chain store cards, oil company cards—any card that will charge you interest if you carry a balance with it.

Second, select the Visa, MasterCard, or Discover card with the lowest interest rate. Set this card aside.

Third, find the sharpest pair of scissors you own. But do not run with them.

Fourth, and quickly—before the evil twin whispers sweet deceptions in your ear—take each card from the pile, insert between scissors, and *SLICE AWAY*. I mean it. Be ruthless. Turn those cards to confetti.

I know, it sounds drastic. Even painful. But any pain you feel is only momentary. Like excising cancerous growths from your arm, you're excising harmful growths from your financial life. It may hurt a bit, but you know you must do it to keep those growths from metastasizing. You're going to halt the sickness in its tracks and get healthy again.

Let me assure you, you are doing the smart thing. Contrary to what your world tells you, *you do not need all these cards.* You're going to get along just fine without them, thank you. You're going to pay off your balances and close these accounts, never to be pulled down by them again. You're going to experience the incredible freedom of being DEBTFREE. Instead of you serving your lender, your money is going to serve you.

Strange as it may seem, shredding your card collection is among the most pivotal steps you can take to improve your financial picture. Don't procrastinate. Do it *now*!

3. REMOVE TEMPTATION: KEEP YOUR SURVIVING CREDIT CARD OUT OF YOUR WALLET

Hopefully you are now looking at (1) one low-interest credit card and (2) one pile of plastic shavings. Do not entertain second thoughts, gasping "What have I done?" as you dash for a bottle of Elmer's glue. You have definitely done the right thing. *You do not need those cards.*

You now have one credit card. This is going to serve as your one card to keep in reserve for a genuine emergency. But it is no longer a license to spend. Therefore, should you carry it in your wallet?

Well, be honest: If you've recently sworn off chocolate, does keeping chocolate in the house help or hurt your resolve? I don't know about you, but chocolate needs a restraining order to keep me away, and even then I'll take on the Denver Broncos' offensive line to get to it. What if you're trying to quit smoking? Fortunately I never started this habit, but my smoker friends tell me that stopping is tough enough *without* cigarettes nearby; if cigarettes are in the pocket, purse, or somewhere in the house, quitting is nearly impossible—the allure is just too tough to resist.

See the parallel? Just as a chocoholic or ex-smoker risks back-sliding if temptation is within easy reach, so we risk backsliding if we carry a credit card. Even though we've now reduced our inventory to one card, the allure is still too strong.

So the next strategy is to *make your one low-interest credit card more difficult to access.* Instead of putting this card back in your wallet, hide it away in a place so inconvenient that you'll be forced to pause and think seriously before using it. Consider

- tucking it in an out-of-the-way cupboard or drawer, or

- keeping it in your safe-deposit box, or

- freezing the card in a water-filled milk carton.

Having to retrieve your credit card before making a purchase gives you a self-imposed "waiting period" in which to stop, regain your wits, and contemplate whether you really "need" a desired item enough to put it on credit. It is truly amazing how a half-day's wait can dissipate the urge to spend.

You're keeping this one low-interest credit card strictly as backup in case of a genuine emergency that you can't otherwise handle from savings. Trip to Disney World? Nice, but not an emergency—save up ahead of time and pay as you go. New DVD system? Also nice, but not an emergency—save up and pay cash. When we refer to a "genuine emergency," we're talking about unexpected but necessary budget-busters such as your obligation on a big medical bill or a major car repair. If your savings reserves aren't sufficient to pay in full for such things, the credit card is there waiting to help you. Once you've used it, just return it to its hiding place, then move heaven and earth to pay off the balance as fast as possible.

4. Carry a Debit Card instead of Your Credit Card

With your sole credit card hidden away, what do you do in those unexpected moments such as when Guido's Pasta Palace won't take a check and you're short of cash? Not to worry, we've got you covered.

Most likely your bank offers either a Visa or MasterCard *debit card,* which looks and acts much the same as a credit card with one wonderful difference: If you pay with a debit card, the expense is automatically deducted from your checking account. Thus it does not accrue interest and does not add to your consumer debt.

Banks usually charge an annual fee for a debit card, but consider this expense an investment in personal discipline; the fee pales in comparison to the high interest you'd pay on credit card balances. On the upside, a debit card can get you through most of the financial surprises that come your way. You can keep the credit card safely ensconced because Guido will honor your debit card just as he would a credit card. So will gas stations, repair shops, and grocery stores. If necessary, you can later transfer funds from savings to your checking account to cover the emergency expense.

Do not, however, use a debit card to excuse excess spending. The natural result will be too much month at the end of the money. Consider it a convenience meant only to bridge those occasions when you don't have sufficient cash in your wallet for a normal expense. Just be certain that (1) you have enough funds in checking to cover the expense; (2) it's an expense your spending plan already calls for; and, most important, (3) you deduct the expense from your checking ledger immediately so it doesn't surprise you when the statement arrives.

WHAT ABOUT CHARGE CARDS SUCH AS AMERICAN EXPRESS, DINERS CLUB, AND CARTE BLANCHE?

Many of us carry American Express, Diners Club, and Carte Blanche cards. These are *charge cards,* which differ from credit cards in that charge-card balances are due in full at the end of each month. Since charge cards do not carry balances and thus do not accrue interest charges, is it OK to keep one of these cards handy?

Depending on your personal spending habits, my response to

this question is a cautious "perhaps." Having to pay an American Express balance in full each month forces you to stay current. You need to overspend only once to realize that, when the bill comes due, you must pay the piper then and there. If you have a charge card and are using it responsibly (i.e., you use it only for budgeted expenses and have no trouble paying its balance in full each month), then a charge card can serve as a helpful, convenient tool in managing your monthly cash flow. There are some potential disadvantages to charge cards you should keep in mind:

- They charge annual fees of $60 or more. But, as with a debit card, the cost may be worth it if it prevents you from paying bigger interest on credit card balances. However, resist all the flattering pitches for more expensive gold, platinum, and other glamorous-sounding charge cards—their benefits rarely measure up to the higher fees.
- As the Visa ads like to tell us, some places don't take American Express or other charge cards, which could be an occasional inconvenience. However, this minor inconvenience may also be a helpful friend, steering us past many "impulse moments" that otherwise may prompt us to spend money we didn't intend to.
- Like a debit card, a charge card could still tempt you to overspend the funds you have in your checking account, requiring you to juggle other resources to make it through the month. So, as with a debit card, use it only as a convenience for normally budgeted expenses—or for a genuine emergency.

5. PRIORITIZE ALL YOUR CREDITORS

List names, phone numbers, the balance owed on each account, the interest rate you're paying, the minimum required payment, and your current monthly payment. As you look over your list, rank your debts from the "most expensive" to the "least expensive" not by the size of the debt, but by the amount of monthly interest you're being assessed. Eliminating highest-interest debts first will hasten the day when interest stops compounding against you and begins working in your favor.

When you've made your decisions, take a clean sheet of paper and list your creditors again, this time according to payment priority.

6. Assign a Monthly Payment Amount to Each Creditor

Your mission is to keep everyone happy while you pay off your creditors one at a time. All creditors except your top priority receive their minimum monthly payment until it's their turn to move to the top. Meanwhile, you're going to send as much as you can every month to your most expensive creditor—*the minimum payment plus at least $50*. If you can possibly send $75, $100, or more above the minimum, do it.

Be diligent about making each monthly payment on time. True, you've made pasta of all your credit cards except one. But you're still receiving monthly statements from each creditor and will continue to do so until you've paid them in full. So never allow a payment to be late, and never make a creditor call you. No matter how deep the hole, you will climb out of it responsibly and with integrity. You'll demonstrate good faith and feel much better about yourself when you're diligent with every payment.

7. Apply Some Found Money

You can knock the wind out of your debt load with a couple of big lump-sum payments, courtesy of any found money that comes along.

Your first source of found money, of course, is personal savings. Many financial experts rightly point out that it makes little sense to keep money in a savings account earning 3 to 5 percent interest while carrying consumer debt of 18 percent. Pay off the consumer debt ASAP and, by doing so, you virtually earn a guaranteed 18 percent on your investment.

However, there's another important side to this argument. Remember your commitment to no more consumer debt? What happens if, as you focus diligently on paying off your debts, Blitzkrieg Murphy enters your life? Wouldn't it be better to handle the Murph from your savings instead of heaping him onto your debt load? For this reason I'd like to see you maintain a minimum of

$1,000 in your contingency reserve even while you're working off your debt. If you have *more than $1,000* in savings, you might take between one-fourth and one-half of that amount and make a lump-sum payment against your top-priority debts.

As we saw in chapter 4, you probably have other sources of found money as well. Now's an excellent time to put those dollars to work. For example, if you were to clean house, basement, and garage and hold a yard sale next weekend, you may earn several hundred dollars you can apply to your top-priority debts. The loose-change strategies themselves could locate an immediate $50 or $60, plus another $30 or so every month that you can devote to debt elimination. Review chapter 4 to see how much hidden money you can apply to becoming DEBTFREE.

With found money, you may find that you can entirely eliminate a debt or two. At the very least, your found money can help you make a significant dent in your top priority. The idea is to make the minimum payment, on time, to every other creditor on your list *while you diligently send as much as possible to your top priority.*

SHOULD YOU USE A HOME-EQUITY, DEBT-CONSOLIDATION, OR 401(K) LOAN TO PAY OFF CONSUMER DEBT?

Many financial publications are quick to recommend that you pay off high-interest credit card debt with lower-interest home equity loans, debt consolidation loans, even loans against your 401(k). Good idea? From a strictly-by-the-numbers perspective, such moves might make sense by trading high-interest debt for lower-interest debt. But there are more important factors to consider.

√ As stated earlier, a house is usually an appreciating asset; thus, it generally isn't wise to use home equity to pay off debt for depreciating or consumable items. In addition, using your home as collateral against consumer debt only places the future of your home in the hands of more creditors. Remember Solomon's words: "If you lack the means to pay, your very bed will be snatched from under you" (Proverbs 22:27). Ideally, if you tap your home equity at all, it should be for appreciating endeavors such as finishing a basement or some other improvement that increases your home's resale value.

With these caveats in mind, consider using home equity to expunge consumer debt *only* if you can exercise the discipline to make it a *one-time, benchmark event* in your journey to financial freedom. In other words, borrow only the amount you need to completely eliminate your consumer debts once and for all. (Resist every temptation to add an extra $3,000 to $5,000 for a trip to Hawaii.) Then, with consumer debts completely paid, swear on the graves of your dear, departed ancestors that you will never, ever build up consumer debt again or deplete home equity to service it.

The advantages of using home equity in this way are (1) all your debts are consolidated into one, (2) your interest rate will probably be lower, and (3) the interest you pay will most likely be tax-deductible. But if you cannot swear on the grave of your dear, departed ancestors, don't take out the loan.

√ Avoid debt-consolidation loans altogether. These are favorites of the financial services industry because, while purporting to decrease your monthly minimum payment, they do so by stretching your payments out forever. Some creditors require minimum monthly payments as low as 1.7 percent of your total balance; factor in the interest, and at this rate you'll be paying for thirty years or more. Good for the lender, bad for you. Follow your nine-step program to do your own consolidating.

√ A loan against your 401(k)? Don't *ever* go there. Plug your ears to all the hype about how you can borrow against a 401(k) or 403(b); the opportunity cost and potential penalties are overwhelming. Whatever your debt situation, consider these tax-advantaged investment accounts *hands-off.* Always keep them growing for your future.

8. Once Each Account Is Paid Off, Formally Close the Account

Once you've paid off an account, your next joyous act is to formally close the account so neither you nor anyone else can use it again. To ensure that it's closed properly, *write* the credit card company requesting that it (1) close your account, and (2) confirm *in writing* that it has done so *at your request*. Keep the written confirmation on file so that, if necessary, you can verify that the account was closed at your behest instead of the credit card company's.

9. Knock Off Those Creditors, One by One

This is no time to become weary in well-doing. You're making progress, but you aren't there yet. As you eliminate one top-priority debt and close the account, move your next most-expensive creditor to the top of the list and shower it with the same number of dollars you'd been paying your first creditor: the minimum monthly payment, *plus $50, $75, $100, or more.* Continue looking for additional found money, both monthly and lump sum, to apply to your top-priority debts. Meanwhile, stay faithful with your other creditors by paying them their minimum payments on time. Stay faithful to yourself by fiercely resisting any new credit spending while you're working so hard to become DebtFree.

STAY DEBTFREE—FOR GOOD!

As you break free of consumer debt, you can count on temptation to try to pull you back in. Even after you've eliminated all but one credit card and hidden it away, even once you've paid your creditors in full, you may catch yourself devising some of the most logical-sounding rationalizations for falling off the wagon.

- "It's on sale! It's too good a deal to pass up."
- "We owe it to ourselves."
- "We'll pay it off with our tax refund."
- "Now that we're almost DebtFree we can splurge a little."
- "Just this once. We'll pay it off at the end of the month."

If you find yourself thinking this way, or perhaps even more creatively, remember that rationalization is what sucked you into the quagmire of debt in the first place. Remember that "easy credit" and "convenient credit" are oxymorons. (I won't point out the second part of that word.) Bottom line: If you can't afford to pay cash today, you can't afford to pay with compounded interest tomorrow.

So ask yourself the tough questions. *Is this purchase a necessity or luxury? Why do I want this? Is it a whim I'll regret in a week? Will I want this item as badly in thirty days when the bill comes?* And when in doubt (say it with me), think DEBTFREE.

It took courage and discipline, but Gary and Rachel turned their credit situation around. The huge monthly sums they had been paying to service high-interest debt are now servicing Gary and Rachel's long-term savings and investments. As they set new goals for their future, it was clear that Gary and Rachel were already feeling a greater sense of security, control, and peace of mind.

The same can happen for you! Stand strong in your commitment. Build on the results for a totally new DEBTFREE life style. It will open so many more vistas for you. You will truly know, deep inside, what it means to be *free of consumer debt—for good.*

TEN

PAY YOURSELF FIRST, AUTOMATICALLY

The Fourth Pillar: *Disciplined, Tax-Advantaged Savings*

Now we put the pedal to the metal.

In earlier chapters we assessed how much money you're likely to need to be self-supporting when Commencement Day arrives. We looked at a baker's dozen of possibilities for locating found money you could begin directing toward this dream. Then we determined how much you should set aside each month—or each year—to make your New Retirement dream a reality. In the last chapter we put you on the road to a DEBTFREE life style to free up even more present and future dollars for your long-term savings and investment programs.

Now it's time to get serious about setting those dollars aside for the future. Time to focus. Time to aggressively harness the power of our seven teammates: compounding, tax deductibility, tax deferral, equity investing, simplicity, diversification, and asset allocation.

"BIGGER, BETTER, AND NOW"

But disciplined saving does not seem to come naturally to most of us. For a nation considered the most prosperous on the globe, the

United States has one of the world's poorest rates of personal savings. From the 1950s through the 1970s, our savings rate ran approximately 11 percent of our gross annual income. Ironically, as we experienced the go-go prosperity of the 1980s and '90s, our national savings rate plummeted to *4 percent or less*—and has languished there since.

Some estimate that baby boomers have saved even less than that—so much stuff to buy, so little time. In our quest for "bigger and better, now instead of later," our personal spending and consumer debt have soared while our personal savings have suffered. We've known all along we'd have to get serious about saving, but we've continued to find excuses to put it off till "someday" . . .

"I'll start saving *when I get my next raise.*"

"I can't save anything *till I get my debts paid off.*"

"Hopefully, *when Christmas is over . . .*"

"We've got some stuff we've been *wanting to get first.*"

"We just *don't have anything left* to save!"

"Someday, *when my ship comes in . . .*"

Do any of those sound familiar? Call them what they are: *procrastination.* Putting off till tomorrow what should be done today. Procrastination is by far the number one enemy of financial freedom.

THE PERILS OF PROCRASTINATION

For the short term, putting off contingency savings can only lead to difficulty and debt whenever we're confronted with the Murphs of life. For the long term, we've seen what the incredible power of compounding can do for your money *when given time— if you start now.* But procrastination dissipates that positive energy by giving fewer dollars less time to work. Ultimately, procrastination leads to a laterlife in which we merely survive when we really want to thrive.

Along with thousands of others, you may be thinking, *But with my bills, there's just not much left to save!* Granted, most costs don't go down, they go up. But together we've already explored dozens of possibilities for found money that may already exist in your life. Now's the time to do whatever it takes to locate and mine that money.

Review the recommended level of savings for your age:

Figure 10.1

AMOUNT OF GROSS ANNUAL INCOME TO SAVE FOR LATERLIFE

Up to age 35	At least 5%
Age 35 to 45	At least 10%
Age 45 to 55	At least 15%
Age 55+	At least 20%

Are you saving enough? If not, it's time to get aggressive—to get ruthless with your budget. Look at it this way: If your employer called you in tomorrow morning and told you he must cut your salary by $400 per month, you would leave no stone unturned to make ends meet. What monthly expenditures could you cut to make it on your new salary? Where would you look for supplementary sources of income? By hook or by crook, you'd find a way to make do on your new salary, wouldn't you?

Now bring that same sense of urgency and resolve to your savings program. You've got to steer serious money to your savings, and you've got to start now. We've helped you find the money. But if, after rethinking and trimming expenses, you're still thinking that there's just not much left to save, then I have another secret for you to discover . . .

THE SAVINGS SECRET

The *problem* is in the *priority*.

In other words, not having much left to save (the *problem*) is rooted in the fact that many of us leave saving until *after* we've paid all our living expenses and bills (*priority*). Inevitably, as Parkinson's Second Law affirms, "Expenditures rise to meet income." Our planned and unplanned spending during the month more than consumes our available money during the month. Just as we do with the act of giving and sharing, we tend to make the act of saving an afterthought instead of a priority.

Fortunately, the solution to this problem is refreshingly simple— so simple that you may not even believe it at first. But trust me; it works. I'm going to illustrate the secret by briefly sharing an example from George S. Clason's classic story, *The Richest Man in Babylon*. He opens with these words:

> In old Babylon there once lived a certain very rich man named Arkad. Far and wide he was famed for his wealth. Also was he famed for his liberality. He was generous in his charities. He was generous with his family. He was liberal in his own expenses. But nevertheless each year his wealth increased more rapidly than he spent it.

How had Arkad come across his great wealth? Had his Great Aunt Brunhilda handed it down to him? Had the Prize Patrol rung his doorbell one Super Bowl Sunday?

His friends posed similar questions. They had gone to the same schools as Arkad, worked just as hard. Yet they were barely keeping their heads above the financial waters. One day they asked him, "Why, then, should a fickle fate single you out to enjoy all the good things of life and ignore us who are equally deserving?"

Arkad was happy to share his secret with them. He replied that he had discovered the foundational secret to financial independence when he realized one simple truth:

"A part of all I earn is mine to keep."

At first his friends laughed, for they had always thought *all* they earned was theirs to keep. But quickly they realized that all their money went to other people—tax collectors, bakers, winemakers, Blockbuster Video—leaving little for themselves.

Arkad, on the other hand, had decided early in his career to *set aside one-tenth of his earnings for future needs and opportunities.* At first it wasn't easy. But after several months it became a habit, and he didn't even miss the money that he set aside. Through a series of experiences he learned to distinguish good investments from bad, and his nest egg grew. All the while, he was generous with those around him.

MOVE TO THE FRONT OF THE LINE

In one simple sentence, Clason, through his lead character, has underscored the foundational secret to successful savings: "A part of all I earn is mine to keep." To make sure he kept a part of his earnings, Arkad *set aside his portion first, before paying any other bills.*

Our problem is that we tend to put ourselves last in line. We pay first for all of our monthly expenses, including debt service, then see if there is anything left for savings. Too often, there isn't. But the key to savings success is to reverse this procedure. Instead of forking out all our funds to expenses and then saying, "Savings? Are you kidding me?" we will route a specific percentage of our income to savings *before we pay any other bills.*

In other words, just as we did with the practice of giving, we're going to move personal savings from afterthought to priority. After you've given some money away, *move to the front of the line.* It's called "pay yourself first," and it's the key to making disciplined savings happen.

If you haven't been giving off the top and paying yourself first, these new disciplines may take some adjustment. I wouldn't be honest if I didn't tell you the first month or two might feel tight. But don't give up. Remember that before young Arkad became the richest man in Babylon, he endured miscues and doubts. It wasn't until he began giving to others from the top of his income, then moving himself to the front of the line, that his finances started coming together. Like Arkad, if you stay resolute you will discover that your budget soon molds itself around your new priorities. Within six

months, I'm confident you won't even miss the dollars that are rout-
ed to giving and savings.

MAKE SAVINGS AUTOMATIC

When it comes to paying yourself first, we enjoy an advantage
that Arkad did not have. He had to set aside his portion *deliber-*
ately. He counted out the denarii, mounted his camel, rode to
United Desert Bank, and deposited the 10 percent in his savings
account. In modern times, we don't have to do all that. We can have
our denarii set aside *automatically,* thus avoiding a bumpy camel
ride as well as the temptation to spend all our money before we
save it.

Saving automatically is good strategy for both your short-term
contingency savings and tax-advantaged New Retirement savings.
For contingency savings, many employers offer the opportunity to
designate a specific amount from each paycheck to be sent directly
to a money market fund. If your company doesn't offer direct
deposits to savings, you can arrange an automatic biweekly or
monthly draft from your personal checking account to the money
market fund of your choice. Your only obligation is to be sure you
deduct the specified amount from your checking account ledger by
the designated day of the draft.

Opportunities to save automatically also abound for your long-
term, tax-advantaged savings. With 401(k)s or 403(b)s, your
authorized contributions are deducted for you, automatically, from
your gross income. With personal plans such as IRAs, you can
authorize your IRA trustee to make regular automatic drafts from
your personal checking account.

Saving automatically makes sure you pay yourself first by doing
the work *for* you. It steers you clear of temptation by directing a
portion of your earnings to savings *before you have a chance to see*
it, touch it, or spend it. Continue this "pay yourself first, automatically" strategy as long as you earn income. For good measure,
whenever extra income comes your way, get in the habit of sending

a healthy portion of that money to savings as well. A portion of *all* you earn is yours to keep . . . so pay yourself first.

And make it automatic.

FIRST: DISCIPLINED CONTINGENCY SAVINGS

As we saw earlier, your first savings priority is to prepare for life's inevitable Murphs by building a contingency reserve. Since you want this fund to be accessible for any emergency, you will keep it completely separate from your tax-advantaged New Retirement savings programs by using a taxable money market fund.

Your aim with this reserve is to build and maintain the equivalent of three to six months' living expenses. Then, whenever Blitzkrieg Murphy snarls in your face with an expensive brake repair, an urgent trip, a big medical copayment, or even a temporary loss of employment, you can get through the situation without having to use your credit card (or, worse, your retirement savings) to pay the surprise expense.

But as we've emphasized, it's not wise to completely postpone your retirement savings strategy (with all its powerful advantages) while you take the necessary time to build a full three to six months' contingency reserve. So we suggested a compromise to cover both bases until your contingency fund is where you want it to be:

❏ First, try to build $1,000 in a money market fund within the next six months. Do not withdraw any of this money for anything short of a real emergency.

❏ As soon as you've built $1,000 in your contingency reserve, steer at least 2 or 3 percent of your gross income to your tax-advantaged retirement savings programs while you continue to build your contingency fund. Continue this pattern until you've built a contingency reserve equal to two months' living expenses.

❏ When your contingency reserve equals two months' expenses, increase your contributions to your tax-advantaged savings incrementally each year until you're making the maximum contribution. At the same time, continue adding to your contingency reserve to bring it up to the equivalent of three to six months' living expenses.

❑ Once your money market contingency reserve is equivalent to three to six months' expenses, you can leave it alone and turn to maximizing your contributions to tax-advantaged savings. If you do withdraw any funds from your contingency reserve, replenish them as soon as possible to keep your reserve at a comfortable level.

THEN: DISCIPLINED, TAX-ADVANTAGED SAVINGS FOR NEW RETIREMENT

With at least $1,000 tucked away in your contingency reserve, it's time to get serious about building your Big Sum for Commencement Day and New Retirement. And, fortunately, this is where your seven powerful teammates come alongside to help make your efforts worthwhile.

How would you respond if a telephone salesperson were to call you at home (at dinnertime, of course) to tell you about a savings vehicle that will pay you an immediate *15 to 28 percent cash return* on your money—*plus* the likelihood of at least *10 to 12 percent annually*? You'd say "Not interested" and hang up, right? You never buy anything over the phone anyway, and this one especially sounds too good to be true.

Now I'm no phone solicitor, and I don't plan to call you at dinnertime unless I can finagle an invitation for pizza. But I can assure you that the savings vehicle described above is not some rich man's tax haven that invests your money in exotic Purple Bora Bora Jungle Parrots. The savings vehicle that offers such good potential results is available to almost everyone, and it's the key to attaining the kinds of Big Sum numbers you and I are aiming for.

QUALIFIED OR NONQUALIFIED?

Tax-advantaged retirement savings plans are otherwise known as *qualified plans*. In moneyspeak, the term "qualified" simply means that the savings plan is qualified by tax law as one that merits tax-advantaged status (i.e., your contributions are tax-deductible and/or taxes on earnings are deferred until earnings are withdrawn). Thus, retirement savings vehicles such as 401(k)s, 403(b)s, IRAs, Roth IRAs, SEP-IRAs, and Keoghs are qualified plans.

A *nonqualified* plan is any account that is not set up under the auspices of a qualified plan. For example, the taxable money market fund you're using to build your contingency reserve is separate from your tax-advantaged plans and therefore is a nonqualified savings vehicle.

We're talking, of course, about tax-advantaged retirement savings programs, which come to you courtesy of Uncle Sam. In a rare display of magnanimity, our government has actually green-lighted *qualified plans* to encourage us to save for our retirement years. (See related box for an explanation of the term "qualified plans.") Uncle Sam provides incentives by making some contributions *tax-deductible* and all earnings *tax-deferred*, which shaves hundreds off our annual tax bills and enables our savings to compound more vigorously.

In addition, virtually every qualified plan can be set up so that *your contributions are automatically made for you*, before you even see, hold, or spend the money. If the plan is sponsored by your employer, he will deduct your designated contribution from your gross salary each payday and send it to your savings plan; this amount is not taxed as part of your income. So as you pay yourself first, automatically, you're also paying less in taxes.

A quick example can underscore the multiple benefits of qualified plans. Gary has a 401(k) plan at his place of employment. This year he'll contribute a total of $5,000 to the plan, or 10 percent of his $50,000 gross salary. (He hopes to increase his contribution to 15 percent over the next two years.) Gary has authorized his employer to direct $192.31 from each of twenty-six paychecks to his 401(k) plan.

Gary and Rachel's combined income puts them in the 28 percent tax bracket. But because the 401(k) is a qualified plan, Gary's $5,000 total annual contribution is *tax-deductible*—so he does not owe income tax on that amount. This virtually gives him an immediate return on investment of 28 percent, or $1,400. Not a bad start!

And the benefits don't stop with the immediate return of 28 percent. Gary has directed his 401(k) provider to place his money in a couple of growth mutual funds that are likely to provide an annualized compounded return of 10 to 12 percent or more. Because these earnings are all *tax-deferred* until Gary and Rachel begin withdrawing the money in their laterlife, he'll be able to keep more money compounding over time.

The tables at the end of chapter 5 demonstrate the positive snowball effect of disciplined, tax-advantaged savings through qualified plans such as Gary's 401(k). That's the effect you and I want to enjoy as well. Let's look at our choices.

THE 401(K)

Uncle Sam didn't think up the 401(k). In fact, it was an alert, thirty-something Christian pension consultant by the name of Ted Benna who developed the idea after spending hours poring over the tax code. Benna designed a test case, jumped it through the legal hoops, and in 1986 Uncle Sam gave it the official thumbs-up. Since then the 401(k), named after the section of the tax code that sparked Benna's idea, has become one of the most sought-after benefits in corporate America.

401(k)s are for employees of for-profit companies. Your employer provides a form on which you authorize him to deduct up to 15 percent of your gross salary from your paycheck. (There is an annual dollar limit that is adjusted every few years, so ask about the current limit.) Per your instructions on the form, each contribution is invested in one or more mutual funds.

But it gets even better. Many employers (though not required to do so) offer programs in which they match your contribution to your 401(k) up to 5 to 6 percent of your gross salary. In Gary's case, his employer matches his contribution 100 percent up to 5 percent of his gross salary, which will provide Gary an additional $2,500 this year. Employer matches are usually on a *vesting schedule,* which means that should the employee leave the company within four or five years of starting the plan, he may retain only a portion of the employer's contributions. A typical vesting schedule might qualify you for 20 percent of employer contributions after one year, 40 percent after two years, and so on until you are 100 percent vested. Of course, you are always 100 percent vested in all contributions *you've* made, along with their earnings.

Some employers allow new employees to begin 401(k) contributions immediately or within their first ninety days; others require a one-year waiting period. Obviously, you'll want to begin funding your 401(k) the moment you're eligible to do so and maximize your contributions as quickly as your cash flow allows.

THE 403(B)

Also named after a section of the tax code (check the tax code the next time you want to name a new baby), the 403(b) is designed for employees of nonprofit organizations. This qualified plan allows contributions of up to 20 percent of gross salary, with annual dollar limits subject to change. As with the 401(k), contributions are tax-deductible, earnings are tax-deferred, and you'll enjoy most of the other benefits and investment opportunities afforded by a 401(k). If you work for a nonprofit organization, take full advantage of your 403(b) savings opportunity as soon as you qualify.

INDIVIDUAL RETIREMENT ACCOUNTS

While Individual Retirement Accounts (IRAs) have been around awhile, they now come in a variety of flavors.

141

The Traditional IRA. Any wage earner, regardless of whether he has a company-sponsored retirement plan, can open and contribute up to $2,000 each year to a traditional IRA. Contributions to this IRA are fully tax-deductible *if you do not have a retirement plan at work*. If you do have a company-sponsored retirement plan, you can still contribute on a tax-deductible or partially deductible basis if your adjusted gross income (AGI) doesn't exceed a specified limit. These AGI limits will increase each year until 2005, when they'll hold at $65,000 for couples and $50,000 for singles. *Anyone* can contribute to a nondeductible IRA, regardless of his or her income, adjusted gross income, or zodiac sign. (Hey, this is government stuff were talking about, so of course it's not simple. These are the same people who produced a 732,000-page Paperwork Reduction Act.)

Because 401(k)s and 403(b)s allow tax deductibility and may also offer employer matching, you'll first want to max out contributions to any company plans before contributing to nondeductible IRAs. But any funds you do put in IRAs will still enjoy the benefits of tax deferral, equity investing, and compounding.

IRAs can be set up through banks, insurance companies, brokerage firms, and mutual fund families. I prefer mutual fund families that offer no-load (no-sales-commission) investments because most banks, insurance companies, and brokerage firms have personal axes to grind, product limitations, transaction fees, and sales commissions. Mutual fund families will even put you on a monthly draft if you request it, giving you the "pay yourself first, automatically" advantage.

The Spousal IRA. This IRA for the "nonworking spouse" also allows contributions up to $2,000 per year. If one spouse has no earned income *or* is not covered by a company plan, couples with adjusted gross income up to $150,000 may contribute to a spousal IRA on a fully tax-deductible basis. As with other IRAs, taxes are deferred on earnings.

The Roth IRA. The new Roth IRA allows couples with adjusted gross incomes up to $150,000 and singles with AGIs up to $90,000 to contribute $2,000 per person regardless of whether they're covered by company retirement plans. The big exception with the Roth is that your contributions are *not* tax-deductible. In exchange for that fine how-do-you-do, you receive a major benefit when you're withdrawing the funds during laterlife: Instead of simply deferring taxes on investment earnings, the Roth IRA eliminates them completely. That's right; your earnings are income tax–free. What you miss on the front end, you more than make up on the back end by compounding earnings over time, then never paying taxes on those earnings.

INVITATIONS YOU PROBABLY SHOULD DECLINE

Your friendly IRS suddenly turns nasty if you withdraw funds from 401(k)-type plans or IRAs before the age of fifty-nine and a half. With very few exceptions, you'll be docked a penalty of 10 percent of the amount withdrawn, *and* you'll pay income tax on that amount.

And the exceptions aren't really worthy of serious consideration. 401(k)-type plans allow you to take out (and pay back) a loan from your account. While this is lauded as a benefit, it's really not a good idea. A loan sets back your savings and compounding momentum; in addition, if you leave or are terminated by your employer, he can effectively "call" the loan, requiring full payback of the outstanding balance within sixty days of your departure. If you don't meet this payback schedule, both the IRS and your company will get *really nasty*. It's just not worth it. Keep your 401(k) intact and growing and, if a loan becomes absolutely necessary in the future, borrow elsewhere.

When it comes to IRAs, you're allowed to make penalty-free withdrawals from traditional, spousal, and Roth IRAs for college costs or up to $10,000 for a down payment on your first home. But as we've stated before and will state again, it's generally not wise to raid your future New Retirement reserves to pay for today's expenses. IRAs do not have a payback provision as do 401(k)s, so withdrawals for even "good" purposes can set you back significantly.

Unless you have at least thirty years to aggressively rebuild your savings, forego all temptations to borrow or withdraw funds from 401(k)s and IRAs.

The SEP-IRA. This stands for Simplified Employee Pension and is designed for small businesses or people who have self-employment income. With a SEP-IRA you can contribute up to 13.04 percent of self-employment income, after deductions, with annual dollar limits subject to change. (Do you get the idea Congress likes to change its mind?) If you have employees, you must contribute the same percentage of their pay to their accounts as the percentage of your pay you're contributing for yourself. Contributions are tax-deductible, investment choices are similar to those of 401(k)s and IRAs, and earnings are tax-deferred until withdrawal.

With the dramatic increase in self-employment and small businesses on the side, the SEP-IRA is worth serious consideration for anyone who earns self-employment income. As with all IRAs, you can set up a SEP-IRA through no-load mutual fund companies.

The Keogh. Another, older plan for the self-employed is the Keogh. Depending on the Keogh program you set up (there are variations to choose from), a Keogh allows you to contribute up to 20 percent of self-employment income to a limit of $30,000 per year. More paperwork is required in setting up and administering the Keogh, but it may be worth your while, especially if your potential contribution surpasses the contribution limit of a SEP-IRA. As with the other investments above, Keoghs can be set up through no-load mutual fund families.

YOU MAY BE ELIGIBLE FOR MORE THAN ONE PLAN

The array of tax-advantaged retirement savings plans can seem confusing to some, but the good news is that you aren't necessarily limited to one plan. Depending on your circumstances, you may be able to combine two or more plans in order to increase your total annual contributions.

GARY AND RACHEL'S COMBO

For example, Gary has the 401(k) program in which his company matches up to 5 percent of his salary. Rachel teaches in the public school system and thus is eligible for a 403(b) plan. Gary and Rachel can

(1) contribute up to 15 percent of Gary's gross annual salary to his 401(k) and receive matching benefits, *AND*

(2) contribute up to 20 percent of Rachel's gross annual salary to her 403(b), *AND*

(3) contribute up to $2,000 each to either traditional IRAs or Roth IRAs. (Contributions would be *nondeductible* since Gary and Rachel participate in company plans, but they can still contribute $2,000 each and reap the other long-term benefits. In Gary and Rachel's case, the Roth is preferable because all its earnings are completely tax-free.)

DICK AND JENNIFER'S COMBO

Let's look at Dick and Jennifer's situation. Dick has a 401(k) at work; Jennifer is a stay-at-home mom who homeschools her young children. Dick and Jennifer can

(1) contribute up to 15 percent of Dick's gross annual salary to his 401(k) and receive employer matching, *AND*

(2) contribute up to $2,000, tax-deductible, to a spousal IRA for Jennifer, *AND*

(3) contribute up to $2,000 for Dick, non-tax-deductible, to either a traditional IRA or a Roth IRA. (In Dick's case, a Roth would again be preferable to a traditional IRA because with Roths all earnings are completely tax-free.)

DON'S COMBO

One more example. Don has a 403(b) plan at his place of employment. He also has a small handyman business on the side, which brings in anywhere from $5,000 to $20,000 per year. Don can

(1) contribute up to 20 percent of his gross salary to his 403(b) plan at work, *AND*

(2) contribute up to 13.04 percent of his net income from his handyman business, *AND*

(3) contribute up to $2,000 (non-tax-deductible) to either a traditional or Roth IRA. (Again, in Don's case the Roth is the likely

way to go, since he cannot deduct his IRA contribution. The Roth provides better back-end benefits because interest earnings are tax-free.)

There's a variety of possible combinations. Because it can be confusing, it's prudent to have a tax professional look over your personal situation and advise you of your options. The fundamental rule, however, is to take full advantage of available tax deductibility and employer matching of 401(k) or 403(b) plans *before* contributing to any of the individual retirement accounts.

THANK YOU, UNCLE

As you've no doubt detected by now, I enjoy poking a little fun at Uncle Sam—he can be corpulent, flatulent, and grossly inefficient. But he's the only Uncle Sam I've got, and I love him in spite of his faults, so I must give him due credit: He's extended a very helpful hand to you and me when it comes to saving for our future. Qualified plans enable us to use the "pay yourself first, automatically" principle. In many cases we can save with tax-deductible dollars. In all cases, our earnings on investment are tax-deferred (tax-free with a Roth IRA), which gives us the potential for significant compounded earnings over time. And we can move our money within a full spectrum of mutual fund investments offering various levels of risk and reward.

So I encourage you to take full advantage of every tax-advantaged plan you're entitled to.

Disciplined, tax-advantaged savings. That's our fourth pillar.

Our fifth, *Investing for Growth,* addresses how to put those savings to work.

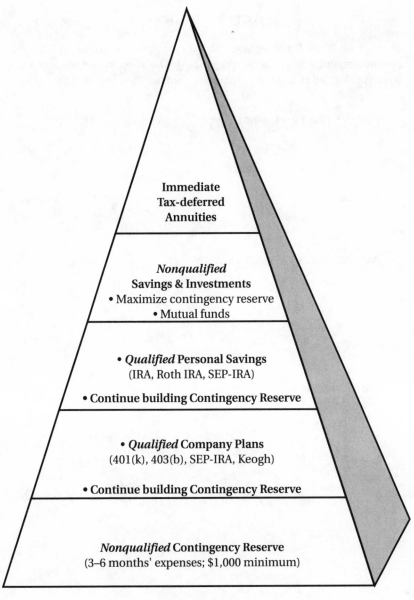

Immediate
Tax-deferred
Annuities

Nonqualified
Savings & Investments
• Maximize contingency reserve
• Mutual funds

• *Qualified* **Personal Savings**
(IRA, Roth IRA, SEP-IRA)

• **Continue building Contingency Reserve**

• *Qualified* **Company Plans**
(401(k), 403(b), SEP-IRA, Keogh)

• **Continue building Contingency Reserve**

Nonqualified **Contingency Reserve**
(3–6 months' expenses; $1,000 minimum)

Figure 10.2
SAVINGS PRIORITY HIERARCHY
Start with the foundation and gradually work upward.

ACTION POINTS

Throughout *Never Retire* we've provided Action Points pages to help you personalize and apply what you're reading. Use these pages to record key steps you feel led to take in preparation for New Retirement.

HABITS I WANT TO CHANGE

-
-
-
-

NEW ATTITUDES I WANT TO LIVE BY

-
-
-
-

ACTION STEPS I NEED TO TAKE

1.
2.
3.
4.
5.

ELEVEN

PUT YOUR SAVINGS TO WORK

The Fifth Pillar: *Investing for Growth*

W hat a difference . . ."
"The tide has definitely turned . . ."

Patrick and Jan are holding recent 401(k) statements. They're both beaming.

They have worked hard to get rid of consumer debt—for good. They've scoured their finances and examined their spending patterns and discovered significant amounts of found money. They've increased their charitable giving. They've tucked away a couple thousand in their contingency reserve.

From the very start of their money makeover, Patrick and Jan have felt an intangible sense of satisfaction that they're "getting their financial act together." But today they're also reveling in the *tangible* reward—they're seeing the difference their strategy is making as they save for New Retirement.

The steps Patrick and Jan took have enabled them to direct more money each month toward their qualified savings plans. That, in turn, has turned up even more savable money from the resulting tax deductions. The funds they're setting aside have been invested in equity investments which, during the past year, have earned approximately 13 percent.

Jan has calculated the difference. "We were paying out almost 18 percent interest on our credit card debts. Now that's gone, and this year we've averaged 13 percent annual earnings with our 401(k)s. So we've virtually earned *31 percent* on our investments!"

The incredible power of compounding. Instead of working *against* them, it's now working in their favor. So are tax deductibility, tax deferral, equity investing, simplicity, diversification, and asset allocation.

To use Patrick's celebratory words, the tide *has* turned. No longer are Patrick and Jan "slaves to the lenders" or even to society's bigger-better-now life style of instant gratification. Now in their early fifties, their financial future is looking brighter. The prospect of never retiring in the traditional sense is growing in its appeal. The more they think about it, the more excited they are about a New Retirement of exploration, adventure, outreach, ongoing education, volunteerism—possibly even some part-time work or a small business of their own.

Their Commencement Day isn't tomorrow, of course. They have at least thirteen, fourteen years to go. And Patrick and Jan may choose to work *beyond* age sixty-five. They don't need to decide now. But what they *have* decided to do has put them on course to spend seniority in *their* way, on *their* terms.

The tide has turned.

Just as it can for you.

ON YOUR OWN, BUT NOT ALONE . . .

The results Patrick and Jan are seeing would not be happening if not for the power of equity investments. Had they merely set their money aside in savings accounts, certificates of deposit (CDs), or even money market funds, they might be earning 4 to 6 percent per year—barely above the rate of inflation. Fortunately, they haven't merely set their money aside; they've *put it to work for growth* by investing in promising businesses via the stock market.

As we've seen, the U.S. stock market has averaged better than 10 percent per year over the past several decades. Between 1994 and 1999 the Standard & Poor's 500 index (which tracks five hundred of the biggest and best stocks) did even better, showing average annual returns of more than 26 percent.

We shouldn't expect this upward trend to continue unabated, of course. As with any investment, the past is never a guarantee of future results, and the market will indeed have its bearish years as well as bullish ones. But the key indicator we're looking for is *performance over time,* and the market's overall history shows that the long-term trend has definitely been upward. In fact, an independent study by Ibbotson Associates of Chicago shows that, over the past sixty years, an investment in the stock market would have earned you *thirty-two times* what the same amount of money would have earned in CDs—for each $10,000 earned in CDs, the stock market has earned $320,000. In addition, over any ten-year period since 1926, stocks have beaten inflation 87 percent of the time while CDs have *under*performed inflation 60 percent of the time.

But what if you don't know much about the stock market?

What if you feel downright intimidated at the idea of placing your hard-earned, hard-saved money at the mercy of those frenzied-looking traders on the floors of the various stock exchanges?

How do you choose stocks to invest in?

One of my favorite TV shows follows an enthusiastic Australian animal-rescue guy who dives into swamps in the middle of the night to wrestle angry crocodiles into a flimsy rowboat. His long-suffering wife sits in the rowboat holding the flashlight, saying things like "Be careful, Steve," and hoping Steve remembered to tape the croc's jaws shut before flinging the beast into her boat. These co-hosts haven't been eaten yet because they're good at what they do. And in practically every show they turn to the camera and say, *"Do not try this yourself. Leave this to the trained professionals."*

151

To you, the world of stock investing may seem like that murky swamp filled with hungry crocodiles. But whether the market seems intimidating or you just don't want to spend the necessary time studying charts and placing buy/sell orders, *the good news is that you don't have to attempt stock market investing by yourself.*

You may be on your own, but you're not alone.

MUTUAL FUNDS 101

Enter the *mutual fund*—the simplest, most cost-effective way for anyone to invest in the stock market and participate in its solid potential for long-term growth.

With mutual funds, you can invest in stocks and bonds with the help of full-time, professional fund managers who do all the research and make all the buy/sell decisions for you. You get diversification across a broad spectrum of promising companies. You can choose different funds to address different investment objectives. And all for an extremely low fee—much lower than you'd pay to invest in individual stocks and bonds.

A mutual fund is an investment company in which investors pool their money with a fund manager to buy shares in the fund. The manager invests the money in a selection of stocks, bonds, or other securities, buying and selling according to his read on individual companies and overall market trends. The gain or decline in value of the securities held by the mutual fund is averaged at the end of each trading day to determine the fund's daily gain or decline per share as well as its daily price per share. If the fund manager sells a security, investors share the capital gains or losses generated by the sale; if a security owned by the mutual fund declares a dividend, investors also share the dividend.

MUTUAL FUND FAMILIES

You'll find most mutual funds residing in *mutual fund families,* which are simply companies that sponsor two or more types of mutual funds. Ideally, a family offers at least one mutual fund for each type of investment objective. Many offer several for each category as well as an array of blended, sector, and money market funds. Four solid performers among the dozens of mutual fund families seeking your business are:

- American Century Investments: 800-345-2021; www.americancentury.com

- Fidelity Investments: 800-544-6666; www.fidelity.com

- Janus: 800-525-3713; www.janus.com

- The Vanguard Group: 800-662-7447; www.vanguard.com

A family of funds enables you to diversify your portfolio within the same family and to shift money from fund to fund simply by calling its 800 number. And virtually all families offer savings programs that help you pay yourself first, automatically.

TYPES OF MUTUAL FUNDS

Mutual funds have become so popular that there are presently more than ten thousand funds to choose from, and more are created every year. Regardless of the number of funds, they all fall within one of three basic types of mutual funds: *stock funds* (ownership or equity investments), *bond funds* (loanership or debt investments), and *money market funds* (*short-term* loanership or debt investments).

WHAT'S YOUR OBJECTIVE?

Branching from the three basic fund types are several categories of funds which invest to meet specific objectives. To illustrate, we'll cite funds from the four excellent mutual fund families listed above: American Century Investments, Fidelity Investments, Janus, and The Vanguard Group.

√ **Aggressive growth funds** buy stock in newer or smaller companies that show promising long-term growth potential. They have higher volatility (upward and downward swings in changing markets) and higher risk, but higher potential reward. Best suited for (1) younger investors who have sufficient time to wait out the inevitable market ups and downs and recover from temporary losses and (2) investors who have their other financial bases covered and can afford to devote a slice of their portfolio to higher-risk investments in hopes of higher return. Examples of good aggressive growth mutual funds include

- American Century Ultra
- Fidelity Capital Appreciation
- Janus Mercury
- Janus Olympus

√ **Growth funds** invest in companies that show good growth potential but are usually better established and capitalized than aggressive growth companies. Volatility and risk for growth funds are moderate to high, depending on the fund and the market, with equivalent reward potential. Almost everyone except older seniors should have a portion of his or her portfolio in growth investments to stay ahead of inflation and to average earnings of 10 percent or better. The proportion allocated to growth can be greater in your early years, then gradually reduced as you grow older. Examples of good growth mutual funds include

- American Century Benham Equity Growth
- Fidelity Blue Chip Growth
- Fidelity Growth Company
- Fidelity Value
- Janus Fund
- Janus Twenty
- Vanguard Index Trust 500

- Vanuard Total Stock Market Index
- Vanguard/Primecap
- Vanguard U.S. Growth

√ **Growth-and-income funds** invest in well-established companies that show potential for continued growth but also spin off income in the form of dividends. These actually did better than many aggressive growth and growth funds during the bull market of the mid-to-late '90s. Because they invest mostly in blue-chip companies, they carry moderate volatility and risk and moderate reward. You'll want to keep a significant portion of your portfolio in the growth-and-income genre, especially as you grow older. Solid growth-and-income funds include

- American Century Equity Income
- American Century Benham Income & Growth
- Fidelity Equity-Income II
- Fidelity Fund
- Janus Equity Income
- Janus Growth & Income
- Vanguard Equity Income
- Vanguard Growth & Income
- Vanguard Windsor II

√ **Income funds,** or bond funds, invest in more conservative securities such as corporate bonds and U.S. government-backed Treasury bills. They offer low volatility, low-to-moderate risk, and low-to-moderate reward potential. Older retirees whose priority is to preserve capital lean heavily toward income funds. Good income funds include

- Fidelity Capital & Income
- Vanguard Intermediate-Term Corporate

- Vanguard Intermediate-Term Treasury
- Vanguard Short-Term Corporate
- Vanguard Short-Term Treasury

√ **Blended funds** take the asset-allocation guesswork from you by combining stocks and bonds in proportions commensurate with the fund's objective. These might also be called "balanced" funds or "asset management" funds.

- American Century Balanced
- Fidelity Asset Manager
- Fidelity Puritan
- Janus Balanced
- Vanguard Asset Allocation
- Vanguard Wellington

√ **International funds** invest in overseas companies to capitalize on the global economy. Some international funds span the globe; others are specific to regions such as Asia, Europe, and South America. Depending on the stated objectives of a fund, it can invest in overseas companies that fit an aggressive growth, growth, or growth-and-income profile. Consider

- American Century 20th International Growth
- Fidelity Overseas
- Janus Overseas
- Janus Worldwide
- Vanguard International Growth

√ **Sector funds** invest in market sectors such as gold mining, healthcare, banking and finance, real estate, high technology—you name it, there's probably a mutual fund for it. These are less diversified so they carry greater risk. Healthcare, for example, has been a strong sector lately because of advances in prescription drugs and in demand for care as people get older. But the healthcare sector could show significant volatility should the federal government pass cumbersome national health insurance legislation. Sector funds are like that—good potential with the right timing, but susceptible to quick turnarounds. Examples of good sector funds are

- American Century Utilities
- Fidelity Select Financial Services
- Vanguard Gold & Precious Metals
- Vanguard Health Care

√ *Index funds* are not actively managed by a mutual fund manager because they are computer-driven to hold the same securities followed by various market indices. An S&P 500 fund, for example, owns shares in the same five hundred stocks monitored by the Standard & Poor's 500 index. It's an easy way to mirror the overall performance of the stock market. Although many fund families are jumping on the index bandwagon, The Vanguard Group originated the concept and continues to lead the field with two of the best funds in the industry:

- Vanguard Index Trust 500
- Vanguard Total Stock Market

√ *Money market funds,* as we've already seen, invest in conservative, short-term debt instruments such as certificates of deposit, commercial paper, and U.S. government securities. *Outside* of qualified plans, a money market fund is an ideal place to build your contingency reserve and save in advance for upcoming expenses. *Within* a qualified plan, a money market fund is a good place to park money temporarily while you're deciding which mutual funds to invest in. Among the best money market funds are

- American Century Prime Money Market
- Fidelity Cash Reserves
- Vanguard Prime Money Market

INSTANT DIVERSIFICATION

As we mentioned in an earlier chapter, mutual funds help to "spread the risk" by giving you instant diversification. Instead of placing all your money in the stock of one company or even three or four companies, mutual funds invest your assets in twenty, fifty, one hundred, or even more companies. You can diversify your investments further by allocating your money among the several different categories of mutual funds such as aggressive growth, growth, growth-and-income, and international as well as among different mutual fund families.

LIGHTENING THE LOAD

You can purchase shares in a mutual fund direct from the mutual fund company, through a discount broker, through your qualified plan administrator, or through a registered investment advisor. Some funds charge sales commissions *(loads)* of anywhere between 2 and 8.5 percent of your investment, which comes right out of your principal. Invest $2,000 and the sales commission alone gives you an instant loss of $40 to $170, which puts you in a catch-up mode from day one.

The better way is to stick with *no-load* mutual funds, and there are plenty of excellent ones to choose from. These are usually purchased directly from the mutual fund company, although more and more registered investment advisors and discount brokers are now offering them. Invest $2,000 and the full $2,000 goes to work for you. Your money is still subject to market price swings, of course, but at least you aren't gouged up front by a sales commission.

You'll also want to stay away from funds that charge so-called

12b-1 fees. These are sneaky *back-end loads,* commissions charged when you *sell* shares in a fund. Most 12b-1 funds phase out the back-end load over four to six years, but that's little incentive to purchase their shares in the first place. There are plenty of top-performing, pure no-load funds for your hard-saved dollars.

ONE-STOP MUTUAL FUND SHOPPING

If you're interested in selecting mutual funds from several different fund families, a *discount broker* can save you the juggle of multiple 800 numbers, multiple confirmations, and multiple account summaries. With a single toll-free call to your discount broker, you can buy, sell, or shift money between mutual funds from a large list of fund families; he will also consolidate all the multiple-family paperwork into one transaction confirmation and one quarterly account summary.

The price for this one-stop shopping is a small fee per transaction and/or a small percentage of your invested assets. Many investors feel the convenience and simplification of discount brokers are well worth the cost; others prefer to deal directly with their fund families and save the fees. If you'd like to consider working with a discount broker, call for information and compare the services and fees of the top three:

· Charles Schwab & Company, 800-435-4000; www.schwab.com
· Fidelity Brokerage Services, 800-544-9697; www.fidelity.com
· Jack White & Company, 800-233-3411; www.jackwhiteco.com.

KEEPING COSTS DOWN

As we all know, there's no such thing as a free lunch. To stay in business, mutual funds do assess investors' accounts for the expenses of doing business. These fees are known as *expense ratios* because they're stated as a percentage of dollars invested. When you receive your quarterly statement, the balance shown is your account value after fees have been deducted. Expense ratios are minuscule considering the professional management you get in return.

But when it comes to expense ratios, not all mutual funds are created equal. Some funds spend too much for the results they bring you. So as you evaluate potential funds, keep in mind that ratios for international stock funds should not total more than 1.5 percent of your investment. Domestic stock funds should charge 1 percent or less, with the emphasis on *less*.

The consistent low-fee leader among mutual fund companies is The Vanguard Group; in recent years the average expense ratio for all U.S. funds was approximately 1.20 percent of the amount invested, while Vanguard's averaged 0.29 percent. (For this and other good reasons, Vanguard is my favorite mutual fund family.) Lower expenses mean found money to you!

AND WHERE DO I FIND ALL THIS INFORMATION?

All of these scintillating facts, plus other information you never wanted to know, are available in a free *prospectus,* which securities law requires fund companies and brokers to offer when you're considering a mutual fund. Prospectuses used to be the perfect cure for insomnia—tiny print, intimidating charts, and language only a Mensa member could understand—but fierce competition has recently forced fund families to make their prospectuses more reader-friendly. Within the first few pages, you'll find information on the mutual fund's investment objective, sales commissions (you want *zero*), expense ratios (you want *low*), investment minimums, fund managers, and historical performance.

You can obtain prospectuses by calling a fund family's toll-free number; most families also let you download product descriptions and prospectuses from their Web sites.

WHAT *TYPE* OF MUTUAL FUND SHOULD I USE?

Most qualified plans offer you several mutual funds to choose from, each with a different investment objective. A typical plan may have

- an aggressive growth domestic stock fund,
- one or two growth domestic stock funds,
- one or two growth-and-income domestic stock funds,
- an income (bond) fund,
- a blended fund,
- an international stock fund, and
- a money market fund.

What percentage of your total savings should you invest in stock funds? How much in bond or money market funds? And *what kind* of stock or bond funds?

When it comes to asset allocation, opinions will vary from advisor to advisor. Much depends on your age, your assets-to-date, and your tolerance for risk. One general (and very conservative) approach has you subtracting your age from 100; the result is the percentage of your long-term savings you should invest in stock funds, with the rest going to bond and money market funds. A tweak of this formula for less conservative investors subtracts your age from 125.

But if you're like most men and women of our generation, you may have some catching up to do when it comes to building your Big Sum. Thus you can't afford to be too conservative. Our Never Retire investment goal is to average at least 10 percent annual return on savings between now and Commencement, then 8 percent or better during the first decades of seniority. To stay ahead of inflation and not outlive our money, we'll always need to be invested for *growth*—more aggressively in our younger years and more conservatively as we grow older.

Figure 11.1 suggests an asset-allocation model that accomplishes the quest for growth while diversifying assets among different mutual fund categories. It also goes from moderate-aggressive in the early years to conservative-moderate in the later years by gradually adjusting the percentage of total assets you might invest in each category.

Figure 11.1

ASSET ALLOCATION

FROM NOW TO COMMENCEMENT—AND BEYOND

YEARS TO COMMENCEMENT	STOCK FUNDS	SUGGESTED ALLOCATION	BOND FUNDS	MONEY MARKET FUNDS
30+ years	100%	30%AG, 50%G, 20%INT	0%	0%
20–30 years	100%	25%AG, 60%G, 15%INT	0%	0%
15–20 years	100%	20%AG, 60%G, 10%GI, 10%INT	0%	0%
10–15 years	90%	10%AG, 50%G, 20%GI, 10%INT	10%M	0%
0–10 years	80%	30%G, 45%GI, 5%INT	15%M-S	5%
1st 15 years after	70%	65%GI, 5%INT	20%M-S	10%
Thereafter	60%	60% GI	20%S	20%

STOCK FUNDS: AG=Aggressive Growth; G=Growth; GI=Growth-and-Income; INT=International. BOND FUNDS: L=Long-term maturities (not recommended); M=Medium-term maturities; S=Short-term maturities.

Peek over Patrick's shoulder for a moment. Patrick's 401(k) plan offers an aggressive growth stock fund, a growth stock fund, an international stock fund, a growth-and-income fund, a medium-term bond fund, a short-term bond fund, and a money market fund. Patrick wants to be moderately aggressive with his investments, and as of today he sees himself working full-time at least another fifteen years. He's chosen the "15–20 years" row from the table, which suggests that he allocate his 401(k) assets as follows:

√ *20 percent* in the aggressive growth fund,

√ *60 percent* in the growth fund or a combination of growth funds,

√ *10 percent* in the growth-and-income fund, and

√ *10 percent* in the international fund.

Since Jan is the same age as Patrick, she can allocate her own 401(k) assets in a similar fashion. They can also use their age-appropriate asset allocation with IRAs or any other long-term savings programs they may have in the future.

A FUND FOR ALMOST EVERYONE

I can't close a chapter on putting your savings to work without telling you about one of the best mutual funds in the world.

As I mentioned earlier, the Vanguard Group is my favorite mutual fund family. Across the board, it is a true no-load fund family with the lowest expense ratios in the business. While I use and recommend other families (including the other three mentioned in this chapter), I really like Vanguard's philosophy of putting the shareholder first by keeping expenses as low as possible. Low expense ratios and no sales commissions mean that more of our savings go to work for *us*.

Vanguard also originated the concept of indexing. They lead the field with a wide variety of index funds, including my favorite growth fund: *Vanguard Index Trust 500*. It's not the flashiest, mind you. And not even the highest-earning mutual fund. As an index fund, it holds shares of the U.S. market's top five hundred stocks as determined by the Standard & Poor's 500 index. There's no manager making buy/sell decisions because the stock selections are already decided. Thus the fund *matches* the S&P 500 performance.

At first this may seem like an investment in mediocrity—until you examine the record. Of all the *managed* stock mutual funds out there, *only 10 percent* beat the S&P 500 over time; *90 percent underperform* the average. Thus, by simply mirroring the performance of the S&P 500, you're likely to come out ahead of 90 percent of all mutual funds—which is precisely what the Vanguard Index Trust 500 is designed to do.

Here's why I particularly like this fund:

- Over the long term, it has stayed in the top 10 percent of all mutual funds, consistently outperforming 90 percent of the higher-expense funds run by fund managers who try to beat the market.

- Its costs are the lowest you'll find anywhere: an expense ratio of 0.18 percent. Many managed U.S. stock funds will run .75 to 1 percent or more, and even other index funds have higher fees than the Vanguard Index Trust 500.

- It is completely no-load.

- Because it tracks the market's top five hundred stocks instead of the broader-based market, its exposure to smaller companies—with their more volatile, aggressive growth stocks—is lessened.

- At this writing, its five-year annualized total return is 26.3 percent, just a fraction under the S&P 500 index. (The fund's small expense ratio accounts for the difference.) This puts Vanguard Index Trust 500 among the top performers of all diversified equity funds.

Always remember that any mutual fund will have its ups and downs depending on its underlying securities and the market as a whole. Because Vanguard Index Trust 500 mirrors a good chunk of the stock market, it will definitely reflect the market's uptrends and downtrends. But because we're in this for the long term, and the market's general long-term trend is upward, Vanguard Index Trust 500 can help you keep pace with the domestic stock market . . . and help you keep part of your growth money among the top performers in the mutual fund industry. Consider this excellent fund for up to 50 percent of your growth allocation.

THE FEELING'S MUTUAL

So now it's up to you.

If you have a qualified plan at work, get all the information you can about the mutual funds available through the plan. Determine your asset allocation using the guidelines we've suggested, then fill out the simple form or call the plan's 800 number to divvy your accumulated savings (and future contributions) accordingly.

For personal IRAs, ask your mutual fund family for descriptive brochures and prospectuses, then allocate your savings with the help of their customer service representatives. While we've focused on four excellent mutual fund families in this chapter, there are many other good fund families to choose from. If you're in a weak IRA with a bank, insurance company, or a fund family whose performance doesn't justify its fees or loads, consider opening an IRA with one of the companies we've mentioned and letting it handle the transfer of funds from your old IRA custodian.

Mutual funds are the ideal tool for putting your savings to work. They combine the benefits of compounding, tax deductibility, tax deferral, equity investing, simplicity, diversification, and asset allocation into a powerful force for long-term growth. They allow the little guy to invest right up there with the big guy—at less cost, less risk, and less hassle. Use them to keep your hard-saved dollars working for you and for your future.

TOP TEN GUIDELINES FOR INVESTING FOR GROWTH

1. Save the maximum amount allowed by your qualified plans. Commit to "pay yourself first" and your budget will reshape itself around your commitment.

2. Use mutual funds to simplify your investing. Forget about individual stocks, bonds, treasuries, or CDs. Forget about the overpriced, underperforming IRAs, mutual funds, and money market accounts offered by banks, insurance companies, and Harry the hot dog vendor. Use only reputable mutual fund families and discount brokers.

3. Use only pure no-load (no sales commission) mutual funds.

4. Use low-cost (low expense ratio) funds. Pay no more than 1.5 percent for international funds and 1 percent for domestic stock funds. Many good funds are available for much less.

5. Don't chase the "hot" funds of the day. Use funds that have posted good results over three-, five-, and ten-year periods.

6. Use funds whose managers have successful track records with the same type of fund over five or more years.

7. Diversify among aggressive growth, growth, and growth-and-income funds during your midlife years. As you grow older, gradually shift your emphasis toward growth-and-income and bond funds—with the emphasis on growth-and-income.

8. Always keep a portion of your assets invested for growth to stay ahead of inflation.

9. Maintain a long-term perspective. Don't let temporary market downswings frighten or discourage you. Stay the course.

10. If at all possible, keep part of your growth allocation in the Vanguard Index Trust 500 fund.

TWELVE

PROTECT WHAT YOU'VE BUILT

The Sixth Pillar: *Asset Protection*

You're driving to work, cell phone in one hand and coffee mug in the other, when the compact car in front of you sees the stoplight and you don't. The police cite you for Driving While Stupid, but that's mild compared to what follows. The other driver sues to the tune of $1 million for severe whiplash injuries as well as burns suffered when the impact spilled his coffee onto his lap.

You're horseback riding with friends when your horse suddenly decides to go bareback. The hard landing plants your tailbone in the tundra, then in a hospital bed for several weeks. You'll be out of work for nine to twelve months—part of that time in a custodial care facility for convalescence and rehab. No income—but expenses through the roof.

It's been raining hard for three days straight. On the morning of the fourth day you awaken to the peaceful sound of water lapping the walls of your basement. Eight inches and rising. Muddy, slimy water. Your basement flooring, walls, furniture, and countless storage boxes are wiped out. You call your insurance company only to discover that most homeowners policies, including yours, exclude damage from flooding. You're stuck with the full cost of repair and replacement.

It's no fun to think about financial catastrophes, but sometimes life hits us with really unpleasant surprises. Painful, expensive ones—bigger than the usual Murphs. These are Murphs on steroids. These are the setbacks that can run into the tens and hundreds of thousands of dollars, effectively depleting the financial resources we've been working so hard to build.

You're working hard for a financially independent laterlife and want to protect what you've built. That's why *asset protection* is your sixth pillar of a financially independent retirement. You recognize that real life is what happens when you've made other plans—that sometimes real-life events can be financially devastating.

Most of us don't have extra millions floating around to cover such setbacks. This is why the insurance industry was born: to pool the premium money of millions of policyholders and compensate those who incur a covered catastrophic financial loss. Insurance companies profit when earnings on premium dollars exceed benefits paid out. We benefit because a relatively small quantity of premium dollars can provide peace of mind and keep a big Murph from turning into a financial catastrophe.

INSURANCE YOU NEED,
INSURANCE YOU DON'T NEED

Unfortunately, the insurance business can also be duplicitous and confusing, skillfully playing upon guilt and anxiety to sell us policies, riders, and extras we really don't need. So as we seek to be good stewards of our present and future dollars it's important that we maintain a savvy balance between the two extremes of asset protection: (1) being *under*insured, unnecessarily exposed to the risk of catastrophic loss; and (2) being *over*insured, wasting money on excessive or unnecessary coverage.

In this chapter we're going to save you some money by shining a spotlight on insurance coverage you *don't* need—you can pull this money from the insurer's deep pockets and put it in your own. We're also going to identify the chief financial risks you do face—and coverage we all should regard as nonoptional as we seek to protect our growing New Retirement reserves. If you're like most readers, you'll probably find one or two areas that need shoring up. Perhaps the found money you gain by canceling unneeded coverage will help cover key areas of risk exposure.

Let's consider those financial risks now and see what needs to be done.

THE TWO GUIDING PRINCIPLES OF WISE INSURANCE COVERAGE

1. Ask yourself, *What could provoke a serious financial setback or even wipe out most of what I've worked so hard to build?* We can't account for every possible catastrophe, but wise insurance coverage for the most common occurrences can keep potentially devastating losses to a minimum.

2. Insure only against major catastrophes, not against minor inconveniences. Self-insure as much as you can by keeping deductibles as high as your contingency reserve allows.

Bottom line: Don't get caught *under*insured against the big Murphs. Some prudent premium dollars now can guard against the loss of hundreds of thousands down the road. At the same time, don't *over*insure and waste big money covering relatively minor risks.

THE DEATH OF A BREADWINNER

Who, if anyone, depends on your present and future stream of income?

That's the fundamental question when it comes to life insurance. Its purpose is to replace your income for dependents who would otherwise suffer significant financial hardship upon your death, for as long as they reasonably expect to remain dependent. Thus you want life insurance to assure your spouse the annual cash flow he or she will need indefinitely and to provide for your children until (and only until) they reach the age of independence. Whether you're a primary, secondary, or coequal breadwinner, you need life insurance if any of the following is true:

- your spouse and/or family depend on your income for every-day needs including food, clothing, transportation, and shelter;

- they need your earnings to help eliminate debt;

- you're planning to pay a big chunk of your children's college expenses from your income;

- you and your spouse are counting on several years' additional income from you to provide for retirement.

The amount of life insurance you need (called *face amount*) depends on your debt, liquid assets, number and ages of children, what you have your heart set on providing, and the number of years your children and spouse would need to compensate for the cutoff of your income. The idea is to provide a lump sum large enough for your surviving spouse to (1) invest at a moderate return and (2) draw from those earnings as needed while leaving the principal untouched until later in life.

Taking into account your present level of savings and investments, your debt structure, and your present living expenses, *aim for a face amount of approximately $100,000 for every $500 in monthly expenses your spouse would need to replace.* It makes for a formidable sum, I know—but it's a necessity if you have dependents and do not have several hundred thousand in liquid funds to provide for them in your absence.

Affording what you need is a bit easier, though, when you shop for the *right kind* of life insurance. *Term* insurance can buy you five to ten times the face amount of *whole life* insurance, which combines insurance coverage with an expensive, weak-kneed "cash value" account. *Decreasing term* holds its premium level while gradually decreasing its face amount benefit. *Annual renewable term* holds its face amount but increases your premium every year. The policy to look for is *level-premium term,* which locks in both the face amount benefit as well as your premium level for the life of the policy.

You'll find the best deals through an independent broker who specializes in monitoring an array of companies for the best policies and prices. Some good ones include Direct Insurance Services, 800-622-3699; MasterQuote, 800-337-5433; David T. Phillips & Co., 800-223-9610; and SelectQuote, 800-343-1985. It's all done by telephone and mail—no salesman will huff and puff at your front door.

Note: Never cancel an existing policy until you have been fully accepted by a new company with a better policy. You don't want to be caught "between insurance" or, worse, be denied new coverage after you've canceled an existing policy.

A MAJOR MEDICAL EXPENSE

If your workplace offers a health plan, that's almost always the most cost-effective way to go. If you're self-employed or in another situation in which you need private medical insurance coverage, you'll quickly find that medical insurance is some of the costliest stuff around—but that doesn't make it any less necessary.

Check your yellow pages for independent brokers who specialize in personal medical insurance coverage. In addition to information on major medical plans, ask for information on Medical Savings Accounts, which allow you to set aside a specified dollar amount each month on a pretax basis and choose your own medical providers. Check also the HealthAxis Web site (www.HealthAxis.com), which allows you to play with plan variables and receive quotes on the spot.

As you evaluate possibilities, keep in mind that you want to cover catastrophic expenses (hence the name *major medical*) but not every little medical contingency. Keep your premiums lower by choosing higher deductibles and copayments.

A DISABILITY THAT INTERRUPTS INCOME

What would you do for income if you were disabled by illness or injury and unable to bring in a paycheck? It's a crisis more common than we'd like to think.

The purpose of disability income insurance is to provide income replacement in the event of a long-term, debilitating illness or injury. Typically, disability income insurance will replace up to 60 percent of your gross income.

As with major medical insurance, the most cost-effective way to attain coverage is through a group plan if your employer offers one. However, many companies do not offer disability, and the self-employed are also on their own. It's insurance I hope you will never need to use, but in the event of a long-term problem, you'll be grateful you made the investment.

Look for the following features:

❑ *Definition of disability.* Accept a policy only if it defines disability as being unable to do the work you usually do. This is called the *own occupation* definition, as opposed to *any occupation.* Why is this important? Well, "any occupation" policies define disability as being unable to work in any occupation. Technically, as soon as you're able to say, "Would you like fries with that?" the insurance company considers you able to work and can terminate benefits. See why you want the policy to come through if you're unable to work at your own occupation?

❑ *Benefit duration.* This refers to the number of years you want benefits to be paid out. The longer the duration of benefit, the higher the premium. You can designate as little as two years, but I suggest a minimum duration of five years since many disabling conditions clear up adequately to return to work within that period of time. You can specify up to age sixty-five to insure against a permanent disability.

❑ **Waiting period.** A *waiting period* is the equivalent of the deductible for auto, homeowners, and medical insurance—it's the time between determination of disability and when benefits begin. The longer the waiting period, the lower your premium, and providers typically let you choose a waiting period of thirty days to a year. If you can, opt for a waiting period of three to six months for better premium value—but only if your contingency reserve is built up to three to six months' living expenses to cover you during the wait.

❑ **Noncancelable and guaranteed renewable.** If a prospective policy requires ongoing medical exams, it most likely can be canceled at the insurer's discretion. Be sure yours specifies that it's noncancelable and guaranteed renewable.

❑ **Residuals and COLAs.** As you're making your comeback from a disability, your doctor may advise you to ease back into your work schedule—maybe half-days or three days a week until you're back to your usual fit 'n' feisty self. A *residual benefit* ensures that you're paid a partial benefit to compensate for the time you're still unable to work. Since many disabilities play out this way, a residual benefit is worth having. A *cost-of-living-adjustment* (COLA) will automatically keep your benefit apace with inflation.

Try these sources for personal disability insurance plans: Direct Insurance Services, 800-531-8000, and Wholesale Insurance Network, 800-808-5810.

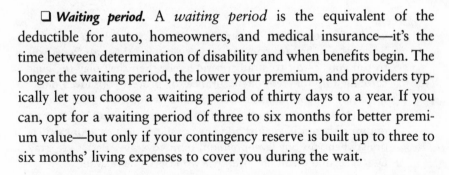

INSURANCE YOU *DON'T* NEED

Life insurance companies make tons of profit on supplementary insurance products because the odds are strongly in their favor against having to pay out. In addition, your cost-per-thousand of coverage is typically much higher than if you were to cover your projected needs with pure level-premium term insurance. Save money by deep-sixing any sales pitches you receive for the following:

◇ **Credit life insurance.** It's ironic—even hypocritical—but hey, it's business. Credit card companies do everything they can to get you to run your credit to stratospheric levels; then they play the guilt card: Sign up for credit life insurance to "protect your loved ones" by paying off your consumer debts "in case something happens to you." (*Now* they care about your financial stewardship.) You'll come out much better if you just add any consumer debt to your calculations when you buy level-premium term coverage. Better yet, stay DEBTFREE, and credit life insurance won't even be relevant.

◇ **Mortgage life insurance.** Before you could take down the "Sold" sign in front of your new home, your lender and every other mortgage company in the universe began pitching term life insurance that will pay off your mortgage if you die. Alas, the math will quickly reveal that these products are rarely the best value. If it's important to you to provide a paid-in-full home to your spouse, figure your outstanding mortgage into your own life-insurance calculation.

◇ **Life insurance on your kids.** Insurers leave logic at the door on this one: "If you love your kids, then you should carry life insurance on them." Hello? The purpose of life insurance is to help replace lost income if a breadwinner dies. Children are rarely the breadwinners; therefore, why buy life insurance on them? Doesn't make sense, except to the insurance agent who pockets the commission.

◇ **Life insurance for singles with no dependents.** The same principle applies here. Who will suffer from the loss of your income if you die? If no one depends on your income, life insurance is unnecessary.

◇ **Flight insurance**. If you're properly covered with your own life-insurance policy, don't let fear or guilt move you to purchase more than you need. Exception: Go ahead and buy some if you notice that the plane you're about to board is missing a wing.

MAJOR DAMAGE TO (OR LOSS OF) YOUR RESIDENCE

If you're a homeowner with a mortgage, your lender requires you to carry adequate homeowners insurance to protect "his" investment. Homeowners insurance typically wraps three types of coverage into one: *your dwelling, your personal property,* and *potential liabilities* arising from the fact that you're a property owner. As with most insurance, the higher the deductible, the lower your premium, so insure against catastrophe instead of the small stuff. Maintain adequate savings in your contingency reserve to pay deductibles and small claims yourself. Be sure these key coverages are part of your policy:

❑ *Guaranteed replacement cost.* Say you bought and insured your home for $150,000 seven years ago but, due to the rising real estate market, it would cost $225,000 to replace that house today. If a tornado or fire suddenly wipes out your nice home, which amount would you rather receive from your insurer: $150,000 or $225,000? A *guaranteed replacement cost* feature pledges the insurer to pay the actual replacement cost of your present home, whatever that cost may be.

❑ *Flood insurance.* The flooded basement we cited at the beginning of the chapter is not a far-fetched scenario. Homeowners policies typically cover water damage resulting from ruptured pipes or water heaters, but no private insurer wants to cover damage due to flooding from outside sources. Which tells you something about how big a risk flood damage must be. If you live near a body of water or a river or a canyon . . . if your home is in a low-lying area that would collect water in a major deluge . . . if basements in your neighborhood are subject to water seepage . . . and particularly if your county has designated your neighborhood a "flood plain," then you should take steps to fill this gaping hole in your homeowners policy.

As we've stated, your private insurer doesn't want to touch this hazard. Fortunately, the federal government stands ready to help with its reasonably priced National Flood Insurance Program. Your insurance agent or broker can supply informational brochures, or you can call the National Flood Insurance Program directly at 800-638-6620.

❑ *Personal property and liability.* *Personal property* is all the stuff you keep inside the house. Usually this coverage is a given percentage of the dwelling coverage. You can purchase optional riders for specific items of value if you like. *Liability* coverage protects you against lawsuits arising from allegedly awful things that happen on your property. If that McDonald's lady spills hot coffee in her lap while sitting in your driveway, she just might sue you over it (it worked once before). If one of the skateboarding Bozinski boys from next door tumbles into your driveway and breaks his face, his parents can sue you—even if his broken nose is an improvement. Homeowners liability insurance covers those and other possibilities. Carry coverage of at least $100,000 per occurrence.

If you rent a home or apartment, your landlord is responsible for dwelling coverage. However, you still need personal property and liability coverage, both readily available in the form of *renter's insurance.* You can buy good policies from the same insurers who provide homeowners coverage.

Homeowners and renter's insurance premiums vary widely for comparable benefits, so comparison-shop at least three companies. AAA, American Family, Allstate, and GEICO are good places to start looking.

DAMAGE TO (OR LOSS OF) YOUR AUTOMOBILE

It pays to shop for car insurance. Rates constantly change, and you'll find that the same coverage can differ among carriers by $200 to $500 per year.

To keep premium costs down, use the highest deductibles you're comfortable with on both *collision* (damage from accidents) and *comprehensive* (damage from other causes such as hail or vandalism). At minimum, take a $500 deductible on each; $1,000 will save you more if you're building an adequate savings reserve to cover such contingencies.

You want to carry *liability* coverage of at least $50,000 per person and $300,000 per occurrence.

Be sure you're taking advantage of discounts for safe driving records, for being over age fifty-five, for multiple cars and multiple policies with the same insurer, for antitheft devices, and for safety features such as air bags and antilock brakes.

Carrying your homeowners (or renter's) insurance, auto insurance, and excess liability insurance with the same carrier can award you a multiple-policy discount, so ask your AAA, Allstate, American Family, and GEICO contacts to propose a package deal.

MORE INSURANCE YOU DON'T NEED

◇ **Dread-disease insurance.** Specialty life insurance policies covering death from dread diseases such as cancer, multiple sclerosis, or accordion music are not good values. What difference does it make *how* you die—you'll be dead regardless. Your necessary face amount is not determined by *how* you leave earth, but by the fact that you leave. Provide what your dependents will need with the face amount of your level-premium term policy—regardless of how you may die.

◇ **TV life insurance.** Forget the TV sales pitches for life insurance for "only $10 per unit," with no medical exam needed. Notice they don't specify what they mean by "unit." Could be $10 per month per $1,000 face amount. Take a calculator to it, or even your fingers, and you'll see how they afford all those TV ads in the first place.

◇ **Accidental death insurance.** Why depend on dying a specific way? Do you really want to be worth more if you die by accident than if you die by natural causes? Again, there's little logic (but much profit) to this rider which insurance agents love to add to your insurance application "for just a few dollars more." If the face amount of your policy is what it needs to be, then you or your loved ones won't have to worry about making your death look like an accident.

◇ **Towing and car-rental reimbursement riders.** Forget riders to your auto insurance policy covering towing and car-rental reimbursement. You'll do better on those with a AAA membership—minus the hassle of filing a claim.

◇ **Extended warranties.** Purchase any appliance today and you'll be pitched an *extended warranty* promising service or replacement if the appliance dies following its manufacturer's warranty. And if you don't buy the coverage on the spot, you're destined to receive multiple phone calls and letters repeating the opportunity. Extended warranties may sound good on the surface, but it comes down to a fundamental question: *Why are they offering to help me in this way?* It's because the odds are strongly in the insurer's favor that he'll never have to make good on his offer and your extra premium dollars can go straight to his daughter's orthodontist. Yes, appliances do go kaput occasionally, but not often enough to shift the odds in your favor. You'll usually come out ahead if you skip extended warranties.

SUE-HAPPY CITIZENRY

If all the lawyers in the United States were laid end to end, it would be a good thing. But until that magical moment, we're left to contemplate all the silly things for which people sue people, recognizing that the next victims of lawsuit larceny could be *us*. We've looked briefly at the basic liability coverage provided by your homeowners (or renter's) insurance and your auto insurance. These are the necessary starting points of good liability coverage. But are they enough?

Unfortunately, in today's litigious society, probably not.

That's where *excess liability insurance* comes in. Excess liability insurance is more casually known as an *umbrella policy* because it provides coverage for just about any kind of personal judgment or settlement not directly related to your employment. It's called "excess liability insurance" because it kicks in once your homeowners/renter's or auto liability coverage has been exhausted. You can carry $1 million in coverage for just a few hundred dollars per year—a bargain few of us should pass up. Another nice benefit of umbrella insurance is that the insurer will most likely provide you with rigorous legal counsel because he doesn't want to pay a judgment any more than you do.

To take advantage of multiple-policy discounts, purchase umbrella insurance from the same provider who insures your auto and residence.

LONG-TERM CARE

We talked about long-term care (LTC) insurance earlier in reference to caring for our aging parents. What's more difficult, at our age, is imagining the need for long-term care coverage for *ourselves*—but it *is* worth considering.

What if that tumble from a horse, traffic accident, fall from a ladder, or even an early stroke were to require *you or your spouse* to stay in a custodial care facility for several months? When you think about it, there aren't many risks that could drain a midlifer's financial reserves faster than a lengthy stay in a long-term care facility. And as we move beyond midlife through our pre-retirement years and into New Retirement, we draw ever closer to the age at which 40 percent of Americans indeed spend some expensive time in nursing homes.

More and more companies are wisely including long-term care insurance as part of their benefits package. If yours does not, consider private LTC insurance anytime after age fifty. The older you are when you buy, the higher your premium—but once you buy in, your premium stays level for as long as you own the policy. (Providers remain entitled to make across-the-board premium increases, such as for every policyholder within a certain state or region.)

Here are some important elements to watch for as you shop for long-term care policies:

❑ *Provider stability.* If you start buying long-term care coverage in your fifties, you want it to be there for you in your eighties, by cracky. Therefore it's important that your insurer doesn't decide to fold up his tent down the road. (Unfortunately, after experimenting with LTC products, a few have done just that and retreated from the LTC business.) As you shop, consider a provider only if it demonstrates two vital qualifications:

(1) It has been dealing in long-term care insurance for at least ten years, and

(2) it is highly rated for fiscal strength by independent watchdogs A. M. Best, 908-439-2200; Moody's, 212-553-0377; and Standard & Poor's, 212-208-8000.

❑ *Qualification for benefits.* Most policies require medical confirmation that your situation is one of three conditions: (1) medical necessity, (2) cognitive impairment, or (3) inability to carry out fundamental activities of daily living. Don't accept a policy that allows the insurance company's hired guns to make that determination. Insist that such confirmation be made by *your* physician.

❑ *Duration of benefits.* Much like a disability income policy, the *benefit period* is the length of time your policy will pay out per nursing home stay. Since the average stay is almost three years, this should probably be the *minimum* benefit period you consider. Unfortunately, many nursing home stays are longer—even lifetime. If your current and future cash flow allows, *lifetime* is the ideal choice.

❑ *Elimination period.* As with disability income, LTC coverage also gives you a choice of how long you'll pay your own way before benefits kick in. Weigh your contingency reserve and other liquid assets against the fact that the average nursing home stay costs approximately $3,500 per month. The longer the elimination period, the lower your premium.

❑ *Inflation rider.* Especially if you purchase long-term care coverage in your fifties, you'll want to include the inflation rider to allow for the upward creep of prices. Look for policies offering an inflation benefit of 4 to 5 percent per year.

Start your research into long-term care insurance by calling two brokers for information and comparative quotes: Bisys Long-Term Care Marketing Group, 800-678-4582, or Long-Term Care Quote, 800-587-3279.

A POSITIVE COMPLEMENT

Granted, it's no fun to talk about hazards, risks, and major exposures to loss. It isn't very exciting to pay good money for products we hope we'll never have to use. Insurance can be a negative topic, which is why it's padded in the term "asset protection." To maintain the right perspective, though, consider the alternative of having no coverage when a catastrophe strikes. With wise insurance choices, you're investing a relatively small number of dollars now so that, whenever a huge, steroid-crazed Murph plants your tailbone in the turf, your dollar loss will be minimized and your New Retirement reserve can continue its undeterred growth for your future.

That's what asset protection is all about. Look on it as a vital complement to our other six pillars of financially independent retirement. With sound asset protection in place, you've taken a big step toward making your money last as long as you do. You're ready to thrive . . . and to soar.

ACTION POINTS

Throughout *Never Retire* we've provided Action Points pages to help you personalize and apply what you're reading. Use these pages to record key steps you feel led to take in preparation for New Retirement.

HABITS I WANT TO CHANGE

-
-
-
-

NEW ATTITUDES I WANT TO LIVE BY

-
-
-
-

ACTION STEPS I NEED TO TAKE

1.
2.
3.
4.
5.

THIRTEEN

I

MAKE YOUR MONEY LAST AS LONG AS YOU DO

The Seventh Pillar: *An Income You Won't Outlive*

How can I be sure I won't outlive my money?"
Ah, the biggest question of them all. The biggest source of anxiety faced by retirees, pre-retirees, and baby boomers contemplating two or three decades of laterlife. You've worked hard and saved hard. Invested as wisely as you can. Covered as many bases as possible with our Seven Pillar strategy. But will it indeed be enough? The last thing on earth you or your children want is for your money to run out before you do.

Which brings us to our seventh pillar of financially independent retirement: *an income you won't outlive.* Here we're going to project ourselves several years (or several decades, depending on your age) into the future to see what financial steps you'll want to take *after* Commencement Day to ensure that your Big Sum lasts throughout your days.

In chapter 2 you made a ballpark projection of your income needs for New Retirement. Since personal circumstances, market conditions, and financial products are subject to change, I encourage you to review and update your projections every year between now and Commencement. But with your present projections in

183

mind, let's move ahead and imagine that you've "shifted gears" from a full-time career to the Never Retire mode. You have no intention of stepping back, sitting down, and waiting to rust out and die. You fully intend to make the most of the rest of your life by growing, exploring, learning, and giving. You're ready for a fresh start, for new beginnings. It's time to seize the day . . . and the decades.

How do you make the money last—while making the most of the rest of your life?

SOURCES OF NEW RETIREMENT INCOME

As we've seen, there are just three fundamental sources of income in laterlife: Social Security (if it's there at all), a corporate-paid pension (if applicable to your situation), and what you can provide (personal savings, investments, continued income). Figure 13.1 capsulizes the scenario:

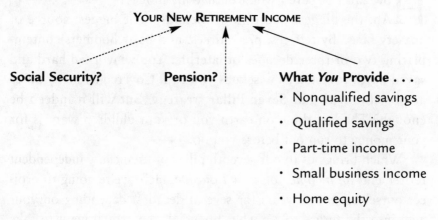

YOUR NEW RETIREMENT INCOME

Social Security?   **Pension?**   **What *You* Provide . . .**
- Nonqualified savings
- Qualified savings
- Part-time income
- Small business income
- Home equity

Figure 13.1
YOUR SOURCES OF NEW RETIREMENT INCOME

As steady paychecks dwindle and your need for monthly or quarterly income becomes clear, you can arrange with your various mutual fund families for systematic withdrawal of funds from both nonqualified and qualified savings plans. As you'll see below, other than your contingency reserve (which you'll try to always keep intact), you'll want to tap nonqualified plans first. Most qualified plans will knock the wind out of you with penalties if you withdraw funds before you're fifty-nine and a half, so you'll want to leave qualified dollars alone *at least* until then—preferably much longer. Keep in mind, too, that our objective is to live off the earnings of our investments during the first several years of New Retirement, leaving our Big Sum intact so it will continue to grow. We're going to try to average a return of at least 8 percent during those years, so we want to limit our annual draw of income to that amount.

Those are the fundamentals. Now let's harness the day-to-day strategies that will help ensure that we're maximizing our money even as we maximize the rest of our lives.

LIVE BY THE LAW OF SOWING AND REAPING

There are lots of good reasons why *an attitude of gratitude* is our central pillar of financially independent retirement; among them is the fact that life's just a lot more fun when we're grateful for it. We can further our joy by turning gratitude into a spirit of giving back. But there's also a very pragmatic reason for the centrality of this pillar—a universal law just as reliable as the law of gravity: *As we sow, so shall we reap.*

Man didn't think this law up—the Creator did! He stated it this way: "Give, and it will be given to you. A good measure, pressed down, shaken together and running over, will be poured into your lap. For with the measure you use, it will be measured to you" (Luke 6:38).

A few years after Jesus spoke those words, the apostle Paul paraphrased the law using a farming metaphor: "Remember this: Whoever sows sparingly will also reap sparingly, and whoever sows generously will also reap generously" (2 Corinthians 9:6).

There is not only wonderful joy in giving, but there is also a practical benefit. God's law of sowing and reaping pledges that if our giving truly flows from hearts of humble gratitude, he will return blessings—spiritual, relational, provisional—beyond our imagination. He takes great joy in replenishing the cheerful giver.

He will provide for you. He will meet your needs. As we consider how to make our finances last through seniority, that's a nice truth to know, isn't it?

START A SMALL BUSINESS—NOW

If you have a hobby or sideline you enjoy, why not develop it into a small business that could provide income well past Commencement Day? Get the start-up costs behind you now, build your sales and goodwill over the next several years, then carry that income stream into New Retirement with you. It'll give you the best of three worlds: ongoing income (which keeps more of your Big Sum compounding for you), the joy of working at something you love (and at your own pace), and the freedom of being your own boss (he may even let you spend mornings on the golf course).

DON'T HANG UP THE WORK SHOES JUST YET . . .

Even if you don't have a small business of your own, you can continue to earn income and stretch those seniority dollars by continuing to work on a full- or part-time basis. More and more companies are realizing the wisdom of hiring "retirees" because seniors tend to bring maturity, reliability, and a solid work ethic to any assigned task. Your commitment to vitality will help you find joy in practically any job you do. You can continue to be productive, use your strengths, make new friends. Work enough hours to qualify, and you can keep taking advantage of group insurance coverage and company savings plans.

CONTINUE TO PAY YOURSELF FIRST

Whether you're in full-time New Retirement or working part-time, you can still set money aside for your future. I know Social

Security and pension recipients who send a healthy percentage of each month's check to their money market funds just to continue the pay-yourself-first discipline. And if they're comfortable with the level in their money market funds, they steer new dollars toward nonqualified mutual funds for better potential return.

See if you can continue to set aside a good portion of any outside income or lump sums that come your way during laterlife. Paying yourself first served you well as you prepared for seniority; let it continue to serve you by helping make your money last.

STAY INVESTED FOR GROWTH

One of the themes we've emphasized in our time together is the importance of always keeping a portion of your savings invested for growth through equity investments.

Our goal during the first several years of New Retirement is to average at least 8 percent annual earnings on our investments and to draw out no more than that 8 percent to live on each year. As you grow older, you'll probably want to become more conservative (unless you're addicted to thrill rides) and aim for earnings of about 6 percent or more per year as you begin drawing from your principal as well your earnings.

Following an asset allocation model such as the one suggested in chapter 11 (Figure 11.1) will help you accomplish those objectives, while gradually adjusting your mutual fund weightings from growth funds to more conservative growth-and-income funds. The key is to always keep a portion of your total invested for growth, which gives you the best chance of staying ahead of inflation while continuing to earn good tax-deferred returns on your invested assets.

KEEP KEY ASSET PROTECTION IN PLACE

Once your Big Sum is sufficient to allow your spouse to live from it the rest of his or her life, you no longer need life insurance.

When you no longer rely on a big paycheck from work, you can cease paying for disability income insurance. In both of these areas you will be "self-insured" since your nest egg can provide the income you need. At age sixty-five you'll also qualify for Medicare health insurance, which offers various coverage options at various premium levels but is far more affordable and less restrictive than private health plans at that stage of life.

Other than these three areas, you'll want to be sure to keep your asset protection in place and up-to-date. Homeowners (or renter's) insurance, auto insurance, excess liability (umbrella) insurance, and long-term care insurance are especially vital as you seek to shelter your finances from the Big Murphs that could swiftly deplete what you've worked so hard to build. Review these policies with your insurer every two years; the premiums you pay are good investments toward helping your reserve last the rest of your life.

BEWARE THE SCAMMERS

You've seen the sad news stories: Another sweet elderly person is cheated of his life savings by smooth, fast-talking scammers. It happens far too often despite ample warnings.

The key to avoiding such atrocities later is to resolve *now*, while we're still younguns, that we will never, ever yield to any opportunity that promises quick 'n' easy money. You've heard it before, but it bears repeating:

If it sounds too good to be true, it probably is.

Sear that advice into your conscious and your subconscious. Resolve *now* that no matter what kind of smooth talk comes your way, whether now or later, you're going to stay the steady course of your Seven Pillar strategy. Ask God to give you a sound mind for the rest of your days and to guide you toward wise choices.

If it sounds too good to be true, it probably is. The only exception we can bank on is salvation. For everything else, it's *caveat emptor*—buyer beware.

DRAW FROM NON-TAX-DEFERRED SAVINGS FIRST

On Commencement Day you're likely to have a combination of *qualified* and *nonqualified* savings programs in place. Qualified plans, as we've seen, enable you to harness the incredible power of tax-deferred compounding (as well as tax deductibility and possible employer matching) while nonqualified savings do not give such benefits. This is why we've recommended that you maximize annual contributions to every qualified plan you're entitled to *before* contributing to nonqualified investments.

As you enter New Retirement and the paychecks diminish, you'll want to draw from any nonqualified savings plans first. Why? Well, doing so will give your qualified reserves more time to work their magic. The longer you can keep money invested for growth in your tax-advantaged plans, the more tax-deferred compounding can help that money grow for your future needs. Keep in mind, however, that most qualified plans (the Roth IRA is a notable exception) establish age seventy and a half as the time you must begin withdrawing income, so you can't keep it all tax-deferred forever. (After all, Uncle Sam wants your tax money *sometime*.) Until then, stretch your reserves by keeping as much qualified money compounding as you can.

GUARANTEE PART OF YOUR INCOME

How would you like to guarantee a stream of income for as long as you and your spouse live? There's a financial product that does just that: the *single premium fixed immediate annuity.*

Test: Say that three times, fast. It's a mouthful, isn't it? But whether you can say it or not, it's a product you may want to consider for a portion of your money as you reach your late sixties or early seventies.

As you grow older, you'll likely want to take fewer risks with your money and lessen your exposure to a cyclical market. This is why we recommend a gradual adjustment to more conservative investments over time—a mix of growth-and-income funds, bond funds, and money market funds. But if your laterlife cash flow is tight, even that much exposure to the whims of the market may keep you awake nights, wondering what (if anything) you can truly plan on. Even if your cash flow is fine, you may still wish to turn part of your Big Sum into a stream of income you can count on regardless of what the stock and bond markets may do.

How Annuities Work

A single premium fixed immediate annuity is simply a contract with an insurance company that guarantees a lifetime income. You put down X dollars from your Big Sum (the *single premium*), and the insurance company pledges to pay you an income of X dollars each month *(fixed)* starting *immediately* (actually thirty days later, for those who pay attention to such things) for as long as you live.

Annuity income is quoted in terms of monthly income per $1,000 committed. For example, if you wish to commit $100,000 of your Big Sum to an immediate annuity, a quote of $8.25 means you'll receive an income of $825 per month. Purchase a $200,000 contract at the same quote and you'll receive $1,650 per month.

- Income payments are locked in and guaranteed for as long as you live, regardless of what the stock markets and interest rates are doing.

- The older you are when you purchase the annuity, the higher your monthly payout—so it's smart to hold off purchasing single premium immediate annuities until at least your late sixties or early seventies.

- In addition, a portion of your income is tax-free since part of it is considered repayment of the principal you paid in.

Just to keep things complicated, annuities come in a variety of flavors—but the only two you need to concern yourself with are *single life* (brilliantly named for annuitants who are single with no designated survivors) and *joint-and-survivor,* for couples.

- **A single life annuity** pays income as long as the annuitant lives; then it's over and done with. No survivors, so the insurer keeps any remaining money. For this reason it pays the best of all the flavors out there.

- **A joint-and-survivor annuity** pays income to the annuitant as long as he or she lives, then an agreed-upon lesser amount, such as 50 to 75 percent, to the designated survivor for as long as he or she lives. Its payout is less per dollar invested because of the bigger commitment on the part of the insurer.

Either way, the single premium fixed immediate annuity provides an income stream you can't outlive. Income-per-thousand will vary from company to company, so it pays to shop around for the best terms. But before you leap onto this bandwagon, there are a few trade-offs you need to know about.

DOWNSIDES YOU NEED TO KNOW

First, while an annuity is guaranteed by the insurer, all bets could be off if that insurer goes out of business. For this reason you'll want to stick to insurers who have earned high fiscal-strength ratings from A. M. Best (908-439-2200), Moody's (212-553-0377), and Standard & Poor's (212-208-8000). It may also be wise to spread annuity purchases among at least *two* highly rated companies.

Second, an annuity isn't easily revocable. Once you commit, the deal is chiseled in granite and you'll pay a hefty penalty to get your money back—if you can get it back at all. Therefore, shop aggressively and read all proposals thoroughly. Plan on locking in to the contracted income stream for the rest of your days.

Third, a fixed annuity may not keep pace with inflation. Eight hundred twenty-five dollars a month today probably won't buy

$825 worth of goods and services ten years from now. So with an annuity you're trading some future purchasing power for the sake of guaranteed lifetime income. One way to mitigate this disadvantage is to purchase a series of annuities three to five years apart in order to lock in enhanced payout rates as the cost of living increases.

Fourth, once you and your spouse are enjoying your eternal reward, the insurance company keeps the rest of your money. That's how annuities work: The insurance company's risk is that it must keep paying you income even if your original purchase amount was used up long ago and you live to be 120. Your risk is that if you and your survivor die before the purchase amount is used up, the insurer keeps what's left. But, hey, you'll be deceased and residing in a place where money doesn't matter, so what difference does it make?

Annuity dollars are dollars you commit in exchange for the assurance of income you won't outlive. Think of it as "longevity insurance," there to help keep your money from dwindling away before you're ready to say good-bye. If the security of guaranteed lifetime income is important to you, it's probably a worthwhile trade-off for part of your New Retirement nest egg. To begin the shopping process, talk with Fee for Service (800-874-5662), a brokerage that supplies quotes on low-load immediate annuities.

THE CHARITABLE THING TO DO . . .

More good news: Instead of enriching the coffers of an insurance company with an annuity, you can help a worthwhile charity through a *charitable gift annuity*. Many nonprofit ministries, organizations, and church denominations sponsor annuities that work much the same as those sponsored by insurance companies. Again, your guaranteed income stream is only as strong as the charity sponsoring the annuity, so do some homework to be sure the organization has a strong history and a promising future.

The added *benefits* of a charitable gift annuity are that (1) your purchase amount may be tax-deductible (if made from nonqualified savings); (2) the charity, not some bloated insurance company, gets the use of your money during the life of the annuity; and (3) if you and your spouse predecease the payback of the purchase amount, the charity (not a for-profit insurance company) keeps the remaining amount and your money makes a positive contribution even after you're gone.

IF YOU STILL NEED MONEY,
TAP YOUR HOME EQUITY

Owning a home free and clear can lend a tremendous sense of freedom to one's financial situation. No mortgage payments! Just insurance and property taxes, and as long as you keep paying those, no one can take your roof and walls away from you. A paid-for house not only boosts your monthly cash flow, it also adds another warm layer to your security blanket.

But what if, after converting all your other savings into income streams, you find you're still coming up short? The same home that's sheltered you thus far may be able to help again.

- One option is to sell your present home and rent an apartment or town house. Gains up to $500,000 are excluded from taxes, so you can tuck 100 percent of your proceeds away for future income.

- You could sell your present home and roll part or all of the equity into purchasing a smaller, less expensive home, reducing your monthly mortgage payments while adding several thousand to savings.

- You could sell your present home and purchase a duplex or triplex. Live in one of the units and rent the other(s) to quiet, responsible tenants. Their rent payments can cover part or all of your mortgage on the building.

What About Reverse Mortgages?

If, as you grow older, you find that your monthly cash flow needs another shot of adrenaline, there's a more dramatic step you can take with your home equity: the *reverse mortgage*. This product is designed for laterlifers whose homes are paid in full or nearly so. You borrow against the value of your home (usually a maximum of 75 percent of its appraised value, depending on the circumstances), and you retain full ownership. The lender pays you a set monthly amount which is not taxed as income because it's a loan. Nor do these payments count against any Social Security, Medicare, or Medicaid benefits you may be entitled to. As with annuities, the older you are, the better the terms and payouts of the reverse mortgage.

The lender continues your payments as long as either you or your spouse continues to live in the house. (You can try collecting after you're both dead and gone, but lenders have silly rules about that.) Here's the key caveat to remember: *Once you're both permanently departed from the house, the loan comes due.* So instead of your children or your estate inheriting the house free and clear, it's likely the house will have to be sold to pay off the reverse mortgage loan. If the selling price is more than the loan's balance, the lender keeps the profit; if the house sells for less than the balance, the lender eats the loss.

Bottom line: If it's absolutely crucial to you that you pass the house along to your children, you'll want to avoid reverse mortgages. However, if at some point you find that the money just isn't stretching far enough, a reverse mortgage may be just the extra boost you need to remain financially independent throughout seniority. Regulations and providers may change significantly between now and then, so stay apprised of the possibilities. Consult local or regional Federal Housing Authority lenders, or call the Federal National Mortgage Association (800-732-6643) for further information.

REMOVE THE PRESSURE: THINK LEGACY, NOT INHERITANCE

In an early chapter I shared why I believe it's inappropriate (or, in the Latin, *tacky*) to plan on a financial inheritance from our parents as if it were an entitlement. The basic reason is that they opened heart, soul, and pocketbook for us all during our growing-up years, and now it's their turn to thrive. Whatever financial resources our folks have set aside since we left the nest are *theirs*—not ours—and they should be heartily encouraged to use what they have to truly *live* the rest of their lives.

An inheritance is a gift—not an entitlement. To mumble about parents spending "our" inheritance is not only presumptuous, it is also the height of self-absorbed ingratitude. They've already given us all they had, all we need, and more than we can ever repay. They should feel absolutely no pressure or obligation to further scrimp or forego their own dreams in order to conserve their estate for us. We're adults now. We're on our own.

You see where I'm going with this now, don't you?

Not only should we free our *parents* of any sense of obligation when it comes to inheritances, but we should also free *ourselves* of the same self-imposed pressure. If we have children, we are indeed obliged to provide them a legacy of love, provision, nurture, character, and a name they can be proud of—but there is no moral or legal ordinance requiring that we leave them a substantial financial inheritance. Indeed, some of the best values we can teach our children are industriousness and self-reliance.

Just as our parents' finances are theirs to live on and enjoy in later-life, so should ours be as we live our own New Retirement dreams. Remove the self-imposed pressure. Don't shortchange yourself by considering a portion of your retirement reserve untouchable because it's "for the kids." It's yours, not theirs. Your true legacy is the set of values you've sought to instill in your children. You reared them with all the love and wisdom you could muster. You taught them to fly; now give them their wings. They're adults now. On their own. If you should spend your last nickel on your last day but leave a legacy of love, you have done your job well.

If you do leave a financial inheritance at journey's end, wonderful! Just don't scrimp through laterlife in order to do so. Don't turn away opportunities for personal growth, ministry, or adventure just so you'll have more to pass along. Let God determine whether your kids receive a financial inheritance and, if so, how much. They already have your true legacy to treasure. Any cash is just icing on the cake.

YOU CAN BE FINANCIALLY FREE . . .

Money. It's only an implement of life, not life itself. But as we've clearly realized, money does matter. We know that wise stewardship is a key to how we live out the rest of our days. We recognize that financial independence is the key to keeping all our options open, to calling our own shots, and to living the New Retirement dream free of dependence on children, government, and charity.

We've shown that you can do it. We've shown you how to build it. And we've shown you how to make it last.

But your money's only as good as *what you do with it.* Throughout *Never Retire,* we've talked not of stepping back, but of stepping up. Not of retiring from life, but of reaching out for more of life. Not of giving in, but of giving back. Not of surviving, but of thriving.

And so we've saved the best for last . . .

PART THREE

THRIVING IN
THE NEW RETIREMENT

14. *LIVE* THE REST OF YOUR LIFE!

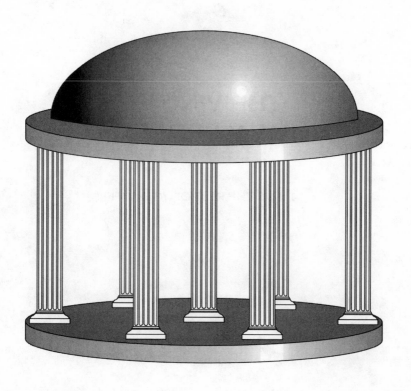

FOURTEEN

LIVE THE REST OF
YOUR LIFE!

The joy of a life fully engaged.

Commencement Day.

The time of new beginnings.

You may be in your sixties, or perhaps you've worked into your seventies. Whatever your age, you've decided it's time. Time to step away from a full-time career. Time to shift gears.

Years back, you determined to never "retire" in the way we've always thought of laterlife. Sure, you'll slow the pace a bit, award yourself more time each day to smell the roses. But you didn't build financial independence in order to spend the rest of your life in the hammock or rocking chair. You're not going to spend the last twenty to thirty years of your life resting and rusting. You've got new mountains to climb, new horizons to explore.

It's the first day of New Retirement.

The first day of the rest of your life.

You're not stepping down; you're stepping up. It's not the time to retreat or give up; it's the time to rejuvenate and give back. There's a whole world out there that needs you. A whole universe you've barely begun to discover. It's time now to seize the day . . . and the decades. Time to join the Psalmist in praying, "Teach us to number our days and recognize how few they are; help us to spend them as we should" (Psalm 90:12, TLB).

So what will you do with your days?

How will you stay young at heart, strong of body, keen of mind?

How will you make the most of the rest of your life?

Rejoice, graduate. It's Commencement Day. You're at the threshold of a whole new world.

Yes, indeed. It's time.

TURN "I WISH" TO "I WILL"

What dreams have you postponed until today—people you've wanted to know, places you've wanted to go, knowledge you've wanted to gain, sights you've wanted to see?

You've lived a good life all along, of course; you haven't exactly put off all your goals till now. But, inevitably, the pace and priorities of life have elbowed aside many of your dreams. They were usually delayed till "someday." Someday I want to visit Alaska. Someday I want to learn a second language. Someday I'm going to write a short story.

Good news. Someday has arrived!

To identify the dreams you may have missed, close your eyes and take a journey of the imagination. Imagine yourself in your midnineties, basking in yet another of God's magnificent sunsets. As the sun ends its day's journey across the sky, contemplate the sunset of your own journey. Look back over good times and bad. Over adventures and accomplishments and lessons learned. It's been a good life, and you're grateful.

But. Any regrets? Any unopened gifts? Opportunities you let pass by? Dreams you didn't pursue?

Maybe you never took a shot at your idea for a small business, although it teased your mind all your life.

Maybe you always wanted to go back to school, take that course in American literature or auto mechanics or music appreciation or zoology.

You may wish you had read more great books. Studied and memorized more of the Bible. Spent more time mastering a skill or nurturing a friendship.

Perhaps you wanted to teach a class or lead a small discussion group, but you couldn't seem to find the time. Maybe you felt led to launch a concerted effort to meet a need in your community, your nation, or your world, but you never quite mustered the courage to act on it.

In the sunset of your imagination, if you look back over your life and find yourself thinking, *I only wish I had tried . . .* then perhaps these are the very dreams you should grasp from the realm of "I wish" and bring back in time—back to the present, back to Commencement Day—and turn into the realm of "I will." Perhaps these are the dreams worthy of your time and energy in the years ahead.

Actor John Barrymore said it well: "A man is not old until regrets take the place of dreams." I think he's right. It's your Commencement Day, the day of new beginnings. Today, choose a dream and give it a deadline. Then give it all you've got. Revel in it.

No regrets.

It's time.

FIND A "MAGNIFICENT OBSESSION"

During midlife and pre-retirement, you may have carved out some time to volunteer for worthy causes. If so, you know something of the humble joy and fulfillment that come from helping others. You may have even discovered your "magnificent obsession"— a passionate empathy, deep in your heart, that makes you long to devote even more of your time, talent, and treasure to meeting a specific need.

I'm convinced we all need a magnificent obsession, especially in New Retirement. God has used our years to give us vast reservoirs of wisdom, knowledge, ability, and experience that are too precious to hoard. He's also created us with the innate need for ongoing productivity and contribution. So now is *not* the time to park those gifts along the sidelines; it's time to shift them into higher gear.

Remember his promise? "Give, and it will be given to you. A good measure, pressed down, shaken together and running over, will be poured into your lap . . ." (Luke 6:38). Nothing will make you feel younger, nothing will cause your spirit to soar higher, than giving your time and abilities to a magnificent obsession. What might that be? Perhaps you already know, and you can't wait to get started. Well, it's time.

If you don't know yet how you might make a difference, see if these suggestions spark some ideas:

- Help build a home with Habitat for Humanity.

- Volunteer to help in your church office during the week.

- Volunteer at your local Salvation Army, Goodwill Industries, or other outreaches.

- Be a small-group leader or Sunday school teacher.

- Volunteer to keep a nearby stretch of highway clear of trash.

- Pass your interests and skills along to the next generation. Teach an elementary-age child how to fish, take pictures, or identify and appreciate wildlife. Teach a junior high student sewing, small-engine repair, painting, or crafts. Teach a high schooler car repair, creative writing, carpentry, or stained glass. What's one of your passions that you can pass along?

- Visit and encourage hospital patients or shut-ins.

- Do gardening or yard work for an ill or disabled friend.

- Help at a homeless shelter.

- Minister to the terminally ill through your local hospice.

- Offer your house-painting or handyman skills to someone who otherwise couldn't afford them.

- Be a host family for exchange students.

- Serve as a volunteer at a local hospital.
- Help friends who need to get away by offering to housesit or pet sit.
- Deliver meals and good cheer through Meals on Wheels.
- Take a literacy-training course and teach someone to read.
- Serve as a spiritual mentor and life coach to a young adult.
- Offer your gardening, yard maintenance, painting, or repair skills to your church.
- Volunteer at a nearby national park, national forest, state park, or museum.
- Help with registration at blood drives and fund-raisers.
- Take your pet(s) to a hospital, nursing home, or convalescent center to brighten a patient's day.
- Read to those who cannot.
- Encourage a teen. Others may decry him every day; let him know you believe in him.
- Volunteer where you're needed most at a parachurch ministry in your area.
- Share your business acumen with young entrepreneurs through SCORE (Service Corps of Retired Executives).
- Volunteer at a shelter for battered women.
- Plant a tree. Consider planting a tree for every year of your life.
- Make teddy bears for children at your local hospital.
- Volunteer (and self-finance) a short-term mission through your church or a parachurch organization.
- Write notes of personal encouragement to friends and acquaintances.
- Participate in annual trail-maintenance efforts at local, state, and national parks.

- Tutor a student in your field of expertise. Math? English? Biology? History? A second language? Pass it on!

- Serve as a wildlife rehabilitator at a wildlife refuge.

- Volunteer at the local zoo or aquarium.

The possibilities are endless. In any corner of your community, there's a need for caring, responsible people—people with time and energy to help light a candle and make that corner a little brighter. You can make a difference. It's time.

COMMIT TO DELIGHT

I shall grow old, but never lose life's zest,
Because the road's last turn will be the best.
HENRY VAN DYKE, "THE ZEST OF LIFE"

Have you ever encountered a crotchety old sourpuss who complained about every ache, pain, price increase, and conspiracy that crossed his mind? Perhaps that's why most of us have feared old age up till now: We don't want to become like that.

Fortunately, crotchetiness is more stereotype than reality. The senior population is no different from the rest of us; for every negative example, there are thousands of wonderful, positive ones. You've come across the positive ones too. They're fun to be around. They endure just as many aches, pains, and price increases as anyone else, but they don't complain. They look for the blessings. Their joy is contagious. When you part company, you feel refreshed.

That's the way I want to be! My outlook is a deliberate decision on my part, a choice of the heart. I can live in discouragement, or I can live in delight. I choose delight. I can grumble, or I can live in gratitude. I choose gratitude. I can litanize my troubles, or I can laugh about them. I choose to laugh.

On this special day, Commencement Day, I encourage you to reaffirm your commitment to joy. You will get so much more out of life when you greet each day saying, "Good morning, Lord!" instead of "Good Lord, it's morning." Continue sharing "two gratitudes" with a loved one each morning or evening. Keep that gratitude journal going. Find something to chuckle or laugh about each day. Life's too short to entertain morose thoughts. (Always has been.) Family and friends are too precious to poison with self-absorbed complaints. (Always have been.) Let your mind dwell on all that's good, and you will be refreshed. Others will be too.

The apostle Paul wrote of joy and delight even as he endured imprisonment. Let me encourage you to read carefully, heed, and even memorize his thoughtful words:

> Rejoice in the Lord always. I will say it again: Rejoice! Let your gentleness be evident to all. The Lord is near. . . . Whatever is true, whatever is noble, whatever is right, whatever is pure, whatever is lovely, whatever is admirable—if anything is excellent or praiseworthy—think about such thing. . . . And the God of peace will be with you. (Philippians 4:4–5, 8–9)

Commit to joy. You'll add years to your life and life to your years. Choose delight. You'll feel better inside and out. And you'll be downright pleasant to be with.

ALWAYS BE LEARNING

The brain is the organ of longevity.
GEORGE ALBAN SACHER (GERONTOLOGIST)

———

I am still learning.
MICHELANGELO

You've learned a lot in your lifetime, including the fact that there's still so much to learn! Like Michelangelo, you'll never retire from the joy and stimulation of learning and creating new things.

You're at the threshold of a wonderful world of new discoveries. You now have more time to explore, discover, experiment, and create. Like a kid entering a candy store, you have hundreds—no, *thousands*—of delectable choices. Here are some ideas to whet your appetite:

- Expand your computer skills. Surf and learn from the Net.

- Create and maintain your own Web site.

- Research and write your family history.

- Join Elderhostel (877-426-8056; www.elderhostel.org), an organization that sponsors dozens of educational seminars and trips nationwide and around the world.

- Design, plant, and tend a flower garden.

- Learn a new language.

- Become a "regular" at your local library. Check out and read at least one book each month.

- Learn fly-fishing or bird-watching.

- At least every six months, attend a seminar on a topic that interests you.

- Go after that undergraduate or graduate degree.

- Go camping.

- Research a Civil War battle, then tour the battlefield.

- Ask your pastor, professors, family, and friends for their choices of the best books ever written. Compile a list of the "100 Best Books Ever Written" and begin reading the books on the list.

- Take a hike. In fact, take dozens of hikes. You'll find them habit-forming.

- Get a good study Bible and read through it once every two years—complete with study notes.

- Learn or improve your proficiency at a recreational activity: golf, tennis, bowling, walking, running, hiking, swimming, skiing—you name it. What have you always wanted to try or improve upon?

- Keep a journal—not just of gratitudes, but of your observations, insights, discoveries, lessons learned.

- Take a Bible class at your church and actually do the homework assignments.

- Learn to play a musical instrument.

- Jump into the arts. Take advantage of adult education classes in photography, painting, stained glass, sculpture, woodwork, crafts.

Don't shut the door on the candy store. Enter, browse, and savor the scents and flavors. Commencement does not signal that learning is over; it signifies that the real learning has only begun. Cross the threshold and partake.

LIVE IN LOVE

Among the lessons we learned from Ebenezer Scrooge is that all the money in the world doesn't mean a thing if we don't love others. He was lonely, miserable, and wretched to be around because he didn't have love in his heart. He was estranged from family and friends because he was too bitter and self-absorbed to reach out in love.

To paraphrase the famous "love chapter" in 1 Corinthians: If we don't love others, we're only making noise. If we don't love others, what good is all our knowledge and abilities? We're worth nothing at all without love. Even if we give everything we own to the poor, and even if we're martyred for our faith in God, these things are of no good whatsoever if we don't love others (see 1 Corinthians 13:1–3, TLB).

I hope you've lived by this creed all your life. But it's especially important now. Set financial independence to the side. Move your acts of giving and learning there as well. If you don't have love welling from your heart, everything else means little. If you don't actively love others, you estrange yourself from the greatest joys and blessings of this world.

But today is the time of new beginnings. Time to rededicate yourself to a life style of love. The author of that love chapter helps us by describing real love:

√ Love is very patient and kind, never jealous or envious, never boastful or proud, never haughty or selfish or rude.

√ Love does not demand its own way. It is not irritable or touchy. It does not hold grudges and will hardly even notice when others do it wrong.

√ It is never glad about injustice, but rejoices whenever truth wins out.

√ If you love someone you will be loyal to him no matter what the cost. You will always believe in him, always expect the best of him, and always stand your ground in defending him.

√ All the special gifts and powers from God will someday come to an end, but love goes on forever (1 Corinthians 13:4–8, TLB, formatting added).

Love goes on forever. Despite everything else we've said, New Retirement will be shallow indeed if we do not treasure and nurture our relationships with our spouses, with our children and extended families, and with our special friends.

KNOW WHERE YOU'RE GOING

The chief end of man is to glorify God and enjoy him forever.
THE WESTMINSTER SHORTER CATECHISM

I believe that statement with all my heart. Can you think of a greater purpose in life? I sure can't. Think of it: The Creator of the whole universe created us to honor him and to enjoy his majesty. Not just here, but hereafter. What a privilege!

But in order to do so, we must do it his way, by his book. The Scriptures tell us he loved us so much that he gave us his only Son. We're told that if only we'll believe in his Son, we won't just wither away to nothingness when we die but will *enjoy eternal life with him in heaven.* (See John 3:16.) It's all so profoundly simple and simply profound that many people—unable to wrap their finite minds around it—reject it. But human beings didn't think this up; God did—because he loves us. Heaven? It's *his* idea. Belief in his Son the way to heaven? I didn't say it; *he* did. He can't lie. He can't be delusional. He's *God.* He is wisdom. He is truth. And his embrace is sure where I want to be, glorifying and enjoying him forever.

Which makes the prospect of growing older and, eventually, passing on much easier to bear. By trusting Christ, I not only enjoy a sense of deep, fulfilling purpose here on earth, but I also know where I'm going when I've breathed my last. I hope your life is filled with the same hope, the same expectancy.

New Retirement is a time to get to know God even better. Time to evaluate everything we think, say, and do in terms of the big question: *Will it bring glory to God?* Time to draw nearer to him each day, to appropriate his love and joy and peace. Time to enjoy him . . . now and forever.

Yes, indeed. It's time.

THE BEST IS YET TO BE . . .

So today is truly the first day of the rest of your life. You've flipped the tassel on your Commencement cap to signify a time of new beginnings—a fresh start. It's time to climb those new mountains and explore those new horizons. Time to step up, reach out, and give back . . . *to make the most of the rest of your life.*

I pray that New Retirement will comprise the best years of your life—years filled with extraordinary joy, vitality, and delight. I hope you'll live each day with such a spirit of adventure that you can join poet Robert Browning in exclaiming:

> Grow old along with me!
> The best is yet to be,
> The last of life, for which the first was made:
> Our times are in his hand
> Who saith, "A whole I planned,
> youth shows but half; trust God: see all,
> Nor be afraid!"

May God bless you as you seize the day . . . and the decades . . . and eternity.

WOULD YOU LIKE HELP
STAYING "ON COURSE"?

LET US KNOW.

As men and women hear about the concept of New Retirement, many have asked if I've considered preparing a monthly newsletter to help them stay "on course" in their journey to a financially independent laterlife. As this book goes to press, some colleagues and I are studying that possibility . . . but first, we'd like to hear from you!

Each monthly advisory would be twelve to sixteen pages packed with up-to-date information and guidance on

- · managing your money
- · saving on taxes
- · investment strategies to build your nest egg
- · mutual fund recommendations and results
- · new sources of found money
- · market and economic trends
- · how new legislation affects you
- · attaining peak health and fitness in midlife and beyond
- · the key decisions you'll need to make between now and Commencement
- · keeping the "Seven Pillar strategy" working successfully

In other words, each month's newsletter would be specially written to continue helping you *make the most of what you've got . . . to make the most of the rest of your life.* If you are interested in such an advisory service, *please drop us an e-mail with your name and address* so we can gauge your interest and keep you informed:

NewRet2000@aol.com

Please feel free to tell us what other issues related to New Retirement you would most like to see addressed in a monthly letter. Once we've made a firm decision to go ahead, we'll let you know how you can become a charter subscriber.